AGGRESSION
IN THE SCHOOLS

THE SERIES IN CLINICAL AND COMMUNITY PSYCHOLOGY

CONSULTING EDITORS:
CHARLES D. SPIELBERGER and IRWIN G. SARASON

AGGRESSION IN THE SCHOOLS

Bullies and Whipping Boys

Dan Olweus
University of Bergen
Norway

**HEMISPHERE PUBLISHING
CORPORATION**

Washington   London

A HALSTED PRESS BOOK

JOHN WILEY & SONS

New York   London   Sydney   Toronto

Hemisphere Publishing Corporation
1025 Vermont Ave., N.W., Washington, D.C. 20005

Distributed solely by Halsted Press, a Division of
John Wiley & Sons, Inc., New York.

1 2 3 4 5 6 7 8 9 0   D O D O   7 8 3 2 1 0 9 8

Library of Congress Cataloging in Publication Data

Olweus, Dan, 1931–
    Aggression in the schools: bullies and whipping boys.

    (The Series in clinical and community psychology)
    Bibliography: p.
    Includes Index.
    1. Interaction analysis in education.
    2. Child study.   3. Sociometry.
    4. Aggressiveness (child psychology)   I. Title.
LB1084.0428   370.15   77-10784
ISBN-0-470-99361-8

Printed in the United States of America

CONTENTS

FOREWORD

Professor Dan Olweus was appointed professor of psychology at the University of Bergen, Norway, in 1970. From 1962 until 1970 he served as the director of the Erica Foundation, a training institute for clinical child psychologists in Stockholm. He received his Ph.D. in 1969 from the University of Umeå, Sweden. Generally recognized as an international authority on aggression, Professor Olweus has made numerous contributions to theory and research in this field. Meeting in Paris in 1976, the International Society for Research on Aggression named Professor Olweus the recipient of its award for outstanding research on aggression, citing as the basis for this distinguished award his work on bullies and whipping boys and his paper entitled, "Personality and aggression," published in the Nebraska Symposium on Motivation (Olweus, 1973).

Professor Olweus's first major contribution to the field of aggression was his monograph *Prediction of Aggression: On the Basis of a Projective Test*, which was published in 1969. This work presented a general conceptual scheme for the determination of aggressive behavior and reported the construction and validation of a projective technique for predicting overt aggression in interpersonal situations. It was reviewed by Professor A. I. Rabin, who described it as " ... a highly sophisticated attempt, methodologically and theoretically, to introduce a semistructured projective method specially devised or tailor-made to assess aggression as a personality trait ... [it] is an exemplary effort that may be emulated by future workers in the new area of projective technology." (1974, pp. 586-587).

The research on bullies and whipping boys on which this volume is based has been published in Swedish, but only a summary of this work ("Personality Factors and Aggression," 1974) has been available in English. Therefore, when I first met Professor Olweus at a conference in Stockholm in June 1975, I encouraged him to consider developing a book based on his research for an English-speaking audience. The present volume provides a detailed exposition of the original work that has been expanded and enriched through the continuing evolution of Professor Olweus's keen theoretical insights and his commitment to empirical research on aggression.

The earlier Swedish book, *Hackkycklingar och översittare* aroused a great deal of interest and caught the attention of the Swedish press and mass media, as well as professional journals in Scandinavia. The remarkable impact of this book on both expert opinion and public policy may be seen in the publication of information booklets for students and teachers, in the recognition of Professor Olweus's research by the ministers of education in both Sweden and Norway, and in reference to this research as a basis for a policy interpellation by the Norwegian Storting (Parliament).

Professor Olweus's work on aggression in the schools is continuing. He is presently engaged in the analysis of interview data with the parents of his subjects and in follow-up investigations of the subjects in earlier studies who are now approaching adulthood. I hope these efforts will lead in time to a sequel to the present volume.

Charles D. Spielberger

PREFACE

The phenomenon to which this book is devoted is an old one. The fact that some school children are frequently and systematically harassed and attacked by other children has been described in literary works, and many adults have personal knowledge of its existence from their own school days. Though many are acquainted with this problem, little effort has been exerted to gain systematic knowledge of it. How prevalent is this phenomenon and what are the characteristics of the pupils who are involved? What factors contribute to the development of such problems in schools? The present book attempts to provide answers to these and related questions.

The Swedish book *Hackkycklingar och översittare*, published in 1973, provides the basis for *Aggression in the Schools*, but additions to and revisions of the Swedish text have been made at many points, notably in Chapters 5, 7, 8, and 9. The empirical data on which the original volume was based were collected in Sweden, but there is no reason for assuming that the problems described and documented in the book are local phenomena or even limited to national borders. The general reactions in Norway and Denmark when the original Swedish research report was published in these countries, in 1974 and 1975, respectively, attest to the validity of this assumption, and discussions with a number of U.S. colleagues have convinced me that the problems also exist to a considerable degree in the United States, as well as in most Western industrialized countries.

Because of the generic importance of the problems under consideration, in writing this book I have endeavored to reach a

broad audience. It is my hope that this volume will be of
interest to educational and clinical psychologists and students in
these fields, to behavioral scientists and psychiatrists, and to
school administrators, school social workers and psychologists,
and teachers and students in education. Judging from the
reactions in Scandinavia, this book may also be of value to
parents of school-age children. I hope that the research described
in this book will contribute to an increased awareness among the
general public of the ubiquity of the problems described, and
that school authorities, teachers, and parents will be alerted to
the need for active preventive intervention.

This volume has been written to permit relatively easy
reading by persons with differing amounts of research training
and experience in the behavioral sciences. For readers who are
not concerned with the more technical aspects of the research,
the following parts of the book are recommended: Chapters 1
and 2, the summarized results of Chapters 4 and 7, and Chapters
8 and 9. The entire book could prove useful as a textbook or
supplementary text for advanced undergraduate and graduate
courses in educational psychology, educational administration,
and personality.

A large number of people—too many to list here—have been
of great help in carrying out different aspects of the research
that is described in this volume and in the preparation of the
manuscript. My warmest thanks to them all. I want to thank in
particular Professors Björn Christiansen, Hans-Jørgen Gjessing,
Gudmund Hernes, and Daisy Schalling and psychologists Barbro
Goldinger, Inga Sylvander, and Barbro Wiking for reading parts
of the manuscript and giving thoughtful comments and suggestions. I am also greatly indebted to Mrs. Judy Messick, M.A.,
who adapted Chapters 8 and 9 from Swedish into the present
edition, and for carefully reading the entire manuscript and
making very valuable suggestions for improvement.

Being a Swede, but working and living in Norway, I have the
pleasure of expressing my gratitude to both the Norwegian
Research Council for Science and Humanities and the Swedish
Council for Social Research for financial support of the research
on which this volume is based. I would also like to express my

sincere thanks to Professor Charles D. Spielberger, one of the editors for this series, for his consistent encouragement and support. It has been a great pleasure working with him.

Dan Olweus

AGGRESSION
IN THE SCHOOLS

1

BACKGROUND AND SOME
DEBATABLE QUESTIONS

This book is about "whipping boy"/"bully" problems, or about "mobbing," among 12–16-year-old schoolboys. It presents a theory sketch of factors that are a priori considered to be of potential significance for the appearance and maintenance of such problems in a school class. A detailed report follows on a research project based on this theoretical sketch. The empirical research leads to a partly new outlook on the problems (Chapter 8), and in the final chapter a program of action is outlined.

It should be stressed that the investigations reported in this book are part of a more comprehensive project concerning mobbing problems. This means, among other things, that I could probably have shed more light on certain aspects of the problems if publication had been deferred until all the material had been analyzed. Two circumstances influenced my decision to present the results from the first series of investigations separately (1973b). In the first place, the results from this part of the project were, on essential points, so unambiguous that there was no reason to suppose that the picture would be modified to any important degree by additional material. In the second place, there appears to be an urgent need for empirical research results in this field, since at the time of publication of my first report (1973b) there were hardly any results bearing directly on the problem.

A FEW WORDS ABOUT TERMINOLOGY

The English expression "mob" has been used for some time in social psychology and sociology, usually to denote a relatively large group of individuals—a crowd or a mass of people—joined in some kind of common activity. As a rule, the mob has been formed by accident, is loosely organized, and exists only for a short time. The members of the mob function side by side rather than face to face, and their identification with the group seldom lasts long. In the social psychological literature, a distinction has been made between several types of mob, including the aggressive mob (the lynch mob), the panic-stricken mob (the flight mob), and mobs arising with the object of obtaining some definite thing, for example certain items of food when rationing is expected (the acquisitive mob). Such sub-division aside, mobs are generally regarded as also having the following characteristics. The members of the mob share such a large degree of (temporary) similarity in feelings, thoughts, and behavior that it is possible to speak of a common reaction or behavior tendency. Further, the reactions of the mob are irrational or, at any rate, the mob functions on a lower and less rational plane than its members would function individually. Last, the members of the mob experience strong emotional reactions (see, e.g., Lindzey, 1954).

The terms mob and mobbing also occur in the study of animal behavior. The Austrian ethologist Konrad Lorenz, for example, uses the term mobbing to denote a collective attack by a group of animals on an animal of another species, which is usually larger and a natural enemy of the group. As an example, Lorenz mentions that a flock of crows will attack a cat or other nocturnal animal if they notice it during the daylight. According to this view, mobbing clearly has survival value for the group: A collective attack may lead to even a large animal being injured or driven away. Moreover, such an activity has the function of teaching the young and inexperienced animals in the group what a dangerous enemy looks like and where it may be found (Lorenz, 1966). Lorenz also describes as mobbing, for example, the action of a school class or a group of soldiers ganging up against a deviating individual (1966).

In the general debate in Sweden, the expressions mob and mobbing have become familiar primarily through the physician Peter-Paul Heinemann, whose article in *Liberal Debatt* (1969/2) was used as a point of departure for a series of articles in *Dagens Nyheter* at the end of 1969. Heinemann's book *Mobbing—Gruppvåld bland Barn och Vuxna* (1972) has, of course, also played a large part in making the terms familiar to the public. The phenomena connected with mobbing have been discussed often and thoroughly in the daily press and the other mass media.

Heinemann does not really provide any precise definition of mobbing in his book, but from several statements in the text and from his examples it is evident that he is thinking primarily of various forms of group violence, usually directed against some individual who does not fit in, that is, the group against a deviant. At one point, he gives this description of mobbing: "Finally a situation arises which can best be described by the expression 'all against one'" (1972, p. 10). He also refers generally to Lorenz's use of the term mobbing mentioned above.

In his illustrations of the various group phenomena, however, Heinemann discusses groups diverging considerably in size, degree of cohesion, emotional state, and attitudes. Mobbing is discussed not only in terms of groups strongly welded together or loosely linked but also in terms of groups that are best described as anonymous masses.

In the general debate, it is primarily mobbing in the schools that has come to the forefront. Here, interest has been centered above all on different forms of collective violence carried out by relatively small and loosely linked groups—usually consisting of perhaps 10–15 children in a class—against a single individual in the class (e.g., Heinemann, 1972, pp. 115–119).

The interpretations or "definitions" of mobbing that have occurred in the press have as a rule implied that a group of individuals (who are alike) attack and torment an individual who deviates from the others. The alleged deviance has usually concerned such external characteristics as being an immigrant, speaking a dialect, being fat, or having an odd appearance or a physical defect, and so forth.

SOME DEBATABLE QUESTIONS

On closer examination, it becomes clear that on certain points there are distinct differences between these ways of employing the terms mob and mobbing and the meaning the expressions usually have in social psychology. Among Heinemann's many illustrations, only the description of the behavior of the anonymous mass is likely to be designated by the social psychologists as mobbing. This divergence from the accepted usage of the concept in psychological circles may not need to be taken too seriously; the fact that an effective term has been coined to describe and draw attention to certain undesirable phenomena may be said to be of greater importance. However, this partial divergence from the social psychological usage may suggest the need for a more precise definition of the term mobbing, or at least more discussion about what phenomena should be referred to by the term. The way the expression has been commonly employed in the general debate—to indicate group violence against a deviant—may lead to inappropriate expectations about the phenomena and to certain important aspects of the problem being overlooked. I shall take up some of these points briefly since they are bound up with the views put forward in this book.

The first point is concerned primarily with the *relative significance of the group versus its individual members.* The notion that school mobbing is a matter of collective aggression by a homogeneous group tends to obscure the contribution made by individual members. Such a view "transforms" the pupils into an almost anonymous band in which all the members—apart from the victim of the mobbing—are animated by the same emotions and strivings. Even if the situation of "all against one" does arise in a school setting (and the chances are that it does now and then), the members of the group probably take part in the activity to very varying degrees. Above all, it is very reasonable to assume that there may be one or a few individuals who take the initiative and who, in a sense, are largely responsible for the situations's arising at all. It is easy to lose sight of the role of such active "bullies" if mobbing is regarded as aggression by a homogeneous, almost anonymous group.

It is also questionable how common all-against-one situations really are in a school setting. The bonds that tie a school class together are normally rather loose, and it is perhaps rather unusual for the whole class (the boys or the girls) to be united in an intense collective activity outside the classroom. Subgroups, cliques, often appear in a class, however, and an aggressive subgroup can probably oppress and harass other children intensely and on a large scale. Such phenomena are easy to overlook if the collective aspects of school mobbing are emphasized too strongly. If mobbing by very small groups is the more frequent type in our schools, the common usage of the concept may lead, for example, to teachers having difficulty in noting the phenomena right in front of their noses.

It is also probable that viewing school mobbing as a group phenomenon related in at least some ways to the behavior of a mass of people may lead to an *overemphasis on temporary and situationally determined circumstances:* The mob, suddenly and unpredictably, seized by the mood of the moment, turns on a single individual, who for some reason or other has attracted the group's irritation and hostility. Such temporary emotional outbreaks from a group of children certainly occur and are, of course, extremely unpleasant for the target. However, I consider it more important to direct attention to another kind of situation, in which individual children are exposed to aggression systematically and over longer periods of time—whether from another individual, a small group, or a whole class.

Finally, the common usage of the term mobbing implies that the victim, the whipping boy, is a deviant. True, there are many examples available in the history of humanity to illustrate that differences in religion, race, or appearance have led to conflicts and persecution. It should not be taken for granted, however, that deviation in race, nationality, or other external factors such as obesity or an unusual appearance is an essential component of mobbing problems. The emphasis in the general debate on external deviations may even have led to other and less obvious characteristics of the victims being pushed into the background. In this connection, Kluckhorn and Murray (1961) may be cited. They pointed out that every person is in certain respects (a) like all other people, (b) like some other people, and (c) like no other person. It would not be difficult to demonstrate, for example, that even a member of a mob is unlike everyone else in the mob in several respects. The essence of this reasoning may be expressed by the question: Do those who become victims of mobbing (if there are particular victims) deviate from those who do not become victims and, if so, in what ways? Light can be thrown on this point as on some of the others mentioned earlier by the empirical research material to be presented later.

FOCUS OF THE PRESENT RESEARCH

As is evident from the preceding comments, I find the common and vague usuage of the term mobbing unfortunate in several respects. However, since the term has become so familiar in Scandinavia through the public debate, I will use it now and then in order to denote generally peer violence and oppression in the school setting. For the sake of clarity, however, it should be emphasized, first, that *my research has focused on the possible presence of, and the mechanisms behind, more serious forms of mobbing, in which individual children and youths (whipping boys) are subjected to physical and/or mental violence and oppression from other children and youths during somewhat longer periods of time.* I judged mobbing of a more temporary and varying character to be of less interest. Second, I have considered the issue of whether those who become the target of violence and oppression are deviant, and in what respects, to be an empirical question, not a definitional one. The same was true of the question of whether the violence and oppression are exerted by an individual person, a subgroup, or a larger group, such as most of the boys in the class. In this context, the possible existence of particular bullies had to be considered.

2

A THEORY SKETCH

At the end of Chapter 1, it was emphasized that in the present investigations, attention has been concentrated on whipping boy problems of some duration—occurring repeatedly and over fairly long periods of time. The reason for this emphasis is that it is problems of this kind that appear to be the most serious: They probably cause the most suffering and may have the most injurious future consequences for the individual. In addition, there are reasonable grounds for believing that light thrown on these problems can provide a foundation for rather general and far-reaching conclusions, assuming that meaningful patterns of results appear.

The choice of such a point of departure means that in both the theory sketch outlined below and the empirical investigations, relatively little weight will be put on more irregular and varying aspects of the environment and the "life" of the school class. This in no way means, however, that more temporary or situational factors do not have a chance of influencing the results, as will become apparent in later chapters.

BACKGROUND MATERIAL

I have already mentioned that research results of direct significance for the problems discussed here are almost entirely lacking. Nor has it been possible to find systematic theoretical formulations to build on. However, some research results, tentative theoretical approaches, and experience that at least suggest the significance of some factors or variables will be touched on briefly.

The term "henpecked" (in Scandinavian languages, a rough equivalent of whipping boy) and its concomitant, "pecking order" have long been used in animal psychology (e.g., Schjelderup-Ebbe, 1922). In its original, limited sense, pecking order denotes the fact that, in a chicken run, there is a rather definite order of rank among the hens, and also that this phenomenon involves a relationship of dominance and submission: The hens do not all peck each other, but in every combination of two hens one pecks and the other is pecked. The pecking order once established is often maintained for long periods of time.

For higher species of animals, such as apes, the expression "dominance hierarchy" is commonly used in place of pecking order. The pattern of social relations is also usually more complex and shows greater variations between closely related species and even between groups within the same species (see deVore, 1968). The dominance hierarchies also often endure for long periods of time among the higher species of animals. The dominating animal or animals have as a rule special functions in the group, for example, protecting its members from external danger. Several factors appear to have significance for the rank position of the individual animal: physical strength, aggressiveness, and sex, and also ingenuity (e.g., in using objects) and ability to gain support from other males of high rank (i.e., among bavians and chimpanzees—deVore, 1965; Hamburg, 1971).

Superficial parallels between the dominance hierarchy in a group of apes and the relations between bullies and whipping boys in a school class are easy to spot. However, delight at finding resemblances leads all too swiftly to overlooking everything that does not agree or that agrees poorly. Thus it is easily forgotten that the basic premises for the existence of a school class are different from those for a group of bavians; the school class has other tasks and other functions. This becomes clear when we consider that the dominance hierarchy among animals is to a large degree regarded as having an aggression-controlling function: The formation of patterns of rank serves to maintain relative social stability in the group, and conflicts and open struggles are suppressed. Thus, although the dominance hierarchy is founded to a large extent on strength and aggression, the consequence is relative peace and quiet in the group.

In bavians and rhesus monkeys *in captivity*, it has often been noted that the dominance relationships take on another character—they become antisocial and destructive for the group. In a zoo, it is not unusual for the group to be ruled by a tyrannical "dictator." Mass attacks on animals of low rank (whipping boys) also occur, something that seems to be extremely uncommon among animals living in natural conditions (Russel & Russel, 1968). According to ethologists, this type of dominance relationship is difficult to understand and explain (e.g., deVore, 1968). It is, however, worth noting that the role of the bully in the group is quite central, and most of the research on dominance hierarchies has been concerned with the position and function of animals of high rank; those of low rank have usually been considered only indirectly. To sum up, it can be said that study of the behavior and social relations of animals—especially those in captivity—seems to offer valuable ideas and angles of approach, but that extreme caution should be exercised in drawing parallels between animals and humans.

For social psychology, the "scapegoat theory" would seem to have most relevance for the whipping boy complex of problems. According to this view, negative attitudes (prejudices) and aggressive behavior directed primarily against minority groups can be understood as a form of so-called displaced aggression: Aggressive tendencies are aroused but cannot be directed against their natural target—they are then displaced on an innocent and usually less dangerous victim, a scapegoat. However, a closer analysis of the theory (see, e.g., Berkowitz, 1962), which appears in more than one variant, reveals several weaknesses and limitations. The results obtained in empirical investigations have also been equivocal or contradictory.

Kurt Lewin and his colleagues (Lewin, Lippitt, & White, 1939; White & Lippitt, 1960) have used the scapegoat notion in their studies of different kinds of group leadership. The three forms of leadership studied have been termed "authoritarian" (or "autocratic"), "democratic," and "laissez-faire." The groups were small (five 10-year-olds in each group) spare-time or hobby groups. In some instances, under an authoritarian or power-oriented leadership, what was termed scapegoat behavior could be noted, that is, an individual member of the group was exposed to "unreasonably" strong aggressive reactions from other members of the group (Cartwright & Zander, 1968). This phenomenon was interpreted as a manifestation of displaced aggression, from the authoritarian, dominant leader to one of the members of the group, who thus became a temporary scapegoat. The results from these group psychological investigations will be discussed in more detail in Chapters 5 and 9. Here, I will point out only that the processes studied by the Lewin group lasted only a short time.

With studies of this type in mind, a theory sketch of whipping boy/bully problems will naturally include relations between the teacher and the class and, of course, relations between the classmates. It may be appropriate to apply to some of these relationships the term employed by the Lewin group and others: the "group climate" or the group's social atmosphere. From similar points of view, it is natural to study the effects of factors such as the size of the school and the class.

A great number of investigations have been carried out in the field of aggression, but it seems as if very few of them are able to throw any direct light on the whipping boy problem. Some of them, however, have a bearing on the behavior and psychological mechanisms of the bully and will be commented on in Chapter 8. At this point, I shall just mention one study that also contains some data on the stability of what may be called whipping boy behavior. In this investigation (Patterson, Littman, & Bricker, 1967), careful observations were made of the behavior of 3-year-old children in two U.S. nursery schools over a period of 8 months. Among other results, there was a surprisingly high degree of individual stability in the amount of aggressive behavior displayed: The children who were respectively high and low in aggression at the beginning of the investigation showed a pronounced tendency to behave in the same way throughout the period. Similar, though less marked, results were obtained with regard to the tendency to be the object of attacks from other children. It appeared, however, that a few children were particularly exposed to aggression from the others.[1]

A great many research results from the field of aggression (see, e.g., Berkowitz, 1962; Olweus, 1973a) indicate the need to consider, in addition to situational factors, the relatively stable personality equipment of each individual. Here, I am also thinking of such factors as genetic dispositions, parent-child relationships, early experiences, and so on, that may contribute to the creation of relatively stable and typical reaction patterns in the individual (personality factors).

Valuable background material was also obtained from several preliminary investigations and from interviews with people having special experience in the complex of problems under discussion. Naturally, the material gained from these interviews showed a good deal of variation as regards perspectives and interpretations, while at the same time a number of opinions were common to all or most people. All in all, the information from these interviews can be said to emphasize the need to take into account several different factors—the peer group, the school environment, the individual, and the individual's home environment.

Of course, the general Scandinavian debate on mobbing has also formed part of the background material.

PRINCIPAL FEATURES OF A THEORY SKETCH

Conceptual analysis of the whipping boy/bully problems resulted in the theory sketch of potentially significant factors, which is reproduced in Figure 1. I shall first describe the various elements composing the diagram and then explain in more detail

---

[1] The median correlation for amount of aggressive behavior displayed in five different periods of observation was .79 in one nursery school ($n = 18$) and .64 in the other ($n = 18$). Corresponding correlations for the tendency to become the target of other children's attacks were .41 and .40, respectively.

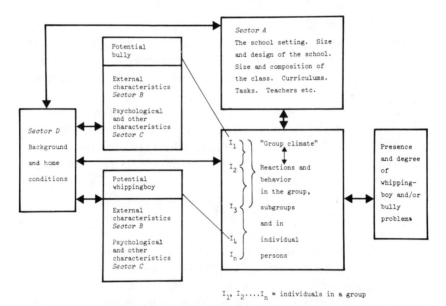

FIGURE 1. Theory sketch of factors of potential significance for whipping boy and/or bully problems.

the connections between the elements. The diagram as worked out here is designed with special reference to a school class, but with slight adaptations it may be employed for other similar groups.

Let us begin with the box farthest to the right—presence and degree of whipping boy and/or bully problems. This is the point of departure, what has to be described and, if possible, explained more fully. The wording "and/or" is used to indicate that in principle these phenomena may occur separately. There may be whipping boy problems in a class without special bullies (this is what has often been called mobbing in the public discussions) as well as bully problems without particular whipping boys. The combination whipping boy and bully problems may also be found and, of course, in certain classes the problem may not exist at all. (The general designation "whipping boy/bully problems" will as a rule be employed in the following chapters, but differentiated terms will be used in Chapter 8). The wording "degree of" is intended to indicate that the problems may occur to a greater or lesser degree in different classes, in more or less serious forms, and/or with many or only a few individuals involved.

The box just discussed is linked most closely with the large box headed "group climate." The symbols I_1, I_2, ..., I_n on the left signify the individual members of the group. Brackets linking these symbols stand for relationships between the individuals, and some of these relationships are summarized in the expression "group climate." In the light of some studies, it also seems natural to link the group climate with the relations with the teacher, that is, with factors or variables in the box above, Sector A. The term group climate is employed in a general sense to signify the degree (possibly also the kind) of tensions and conflicts that may characterize the group as a whole or a large part of it.[2]

It can thus be assumed that the group climate—as well as the individuals' reactions and behavior—may be related to various factors in the school setting (Sector A in the figure): perhaps with factors such as the size of the school and its design; with the size of the class and its composition; with the way in which the teacher conducts the work of the class; with the teacher's personality and satisfaction with the work; with the demands, tasks, and conflicts that school work and the "role" of pupil generally entail.

However, it is not only such structural or system variables in the school environment that can be assumed to have significance. The actual individuals making up the class and potential subgroups may also influence the peer relations, both in the class as a whole and in smaller units of the class. This is indicated in the figure in two ways, by the use of brackets around the individuals and by means of the boxes headed "Potential bully" and "Potential whipping boy." (The boxes Potential bully, I_1, and Potential whipping boy, I_4, are, so to speak, only "lifted out" of the large box.) To enlarge on this

---

[2] From the point of view of group psychology, it might be tempting to introduce additional concepts into the theory sketch, for example, group norms with inhibiting or facilitating effects (see, e.g., Cartwright & Zander, 1968; Shaw, 1971). It hardly seems necessary, however, to give group norms status as a separate concept in the theory sketch. To the extent that relevant group norms exist in the different classes, there are grounds for assuming that they are captured in certain indicators of the group climate employed in the empirical investigations (see Chapter 5).

point, I assume that many classes contain pupils with special characteristics that predispose them to become, under certain conditions, either whipping boys or bullies. These characteristics may be external: As mentioned in Chapter 1, external deviations have often been regarded as playing an essential part when whipping boy problems arise. This kind of characteristic is given a special sector in the figure—Sector B. Further, it is highly probable that psychological and behavior characteristics are of importance—these characteristics are designated as Sector C. I shall not go into detail now about such conceivable character- istics; they will be explored in connection with the empirical investigations further on in the book. Here I will only emphasize that the individual's relation to aggression and violence can be assumed to be an essential aspect of the problem. Of course, several different types of psychological mechanisms are con- ceivable, but the denomination itself suggests aggression prob- lems of some kind, especially with regard to the bullies. Characteristics that reflect information about the attitude or behavior of others toward an individual, for instance, how popular a pupil is among the rest of the class, also fall naturally into Sector C. It can thus be assumed that some pupils have special characteristics that increase their probability of becoming whipping boys or bullies and, consequently, the probability of whipping boy/bully problems arising in the class. However, not all potential whipping boys or bullies actually become the one or the other. Other factors may also be presumed to have significance. The terms whipping boy and bully will be em- ployed only when there is evidence that the problems have lasted some time.

It is natural to pass on from the individual characteristics of the type just discussed to the box on the left—background and home conditions, Sector D. The characteristics that can be assumed to distinguish potential or actual whipping boys and bullies probably have some basis in earlier experiences, in relations with parents or siblings or, to put it briefly, in the developmental history of the individual. There may also be characteristics that are connected with the education, age, and social group of the parents. Current relations with parents as well as with one or more of the teachers—influence from Sector

A, as suggested earlier—may also be of significance for the characteristics in Sector C. The effects of these kinds of factors are obviously not limited to whipping boys or bullies, and this point is illustrated in the figure by the links between the large box $(I_1, I_2,$ etc.) and Sectors A and D.

Summary

I have now described the principal elements in the figure and suggested certain links between the various parts. Some summarizing and integrating comments are in order.

In a group such as a school class, a number of problems, conflicts, and tensions of varying kinds and origin will normally occur. It can be assumed that classes differ considerably in these respects. The interplay between the individuals (the group climate) may be related to the needs and behavior of the individual pupils—the class may, for instance, have a high proportion of individuals with a pronounced need to get praised, to be in the center of things and dominate. It may also be linked with different factors in the school setting, for example, marked antagonisms toward the main teacher[3] or a negative attitude toward the school and schoolwork (Sector A). It is quite conceivable that marked conflicts and tensions in a class will lead to whipping boy/bully problems, or, put somewhat differently, will increase the probability of such problems arising or make them more pronounced.

In the preceding paragraph, the class (or the boys or the girls) was considered more or less as a unit. I assume, however, that single individuals or subgroups can also play a significant role. Accordingly, the presence of one or more potential bullies in a class will increase the likelihood of whipping boy/bully problems arising or make them more marked. A certain form of aggressive self-assertion may be one of the characteristics that distinguish the potential bully (Sector C).

[3] In the lower grades (1-6) in Swedish schools, *one* teacher (female or male) has the main administrative responsibility for each class and does most of the teaching of the class, often 20 periods a week. This teacher will be called the *main teacher* in this book. After grade 6, each class still has a main teacher, but the teaching is gradually distributed among several teachers.

The same reasoning may be applied to potential whipping boys. The presence of one or more potential whipping boys in a class may increase the probability of whipping boy problems arising or make them more pronounced. The special characteristics of a potential whipping boy may be both psychological (Sector C) and physical (Sector B).

The main factors discussed above could, of course, be integrated in a structured theory, and specific hypotheses could be formulated. However, a sound basis for the construction of this kind of formal theory is lacking at the present stage of research. The chief aim in constructing the present theory sketch is to give a preliminary overview of the complex of problems, as a guide to empirical research and analyses. It serves as a starting point or conceptual framework providing some guarantee that essential aspects of the problems will not be overlooked in the empirical investigations. An appraisal of the relative importance of different factors and their interaction can, of course, be made on a safer basis after some research results have been presented.

Further Comments

Figure 1 shows a number of double-headed arrows between the boxes. They are intended to suggest that communication and influence may occur in both directions. Thus it is natural to suppose that parents (Sector D) have some influence on their children—greater or lesser according to the child's age and the special circumstances—but also conversely that the child's reactions and behavior affect the parents. In the same way, the appearance of pronounced whipping boy/bully problems in a class can be assumed to have certain effects on the pupils in the class, not just on those particularly exposed but possibly also on others. The connection between Sector D and Sector A concerns direct and indirect contact and influence between home and school.

The location of a particular factor in the theory sketch may occasionally be a matter for discussion. This applies, for instance, to the factor "composition of the class," which is, of course, determined by the individuals making up the class and by their characteristics—that is, it forms part of the large box in

Figure 1. At the same time, there is, in principle, the possibility of deliberately varying the composition of the class in accordance with special criteria, and this circumstance makes it natural to put composition as a separate factor in Sector A. In a way, this factor is represented twice in the figure. This point underlines a feature common to most diagrams, including the one in Figure 1: The diagram gives only a rough and partial representation of what the author wishes to convey.

Expressions such as "aggressive" and "aggression" have already occurred in the text and will appear again. In the aggressive motive area, various expressions and concepts may be found—aggressive behavior, aggressive impulses or tendencies, instrumental and hostile aggression, and so on—employed by different authors with slightly differing meanings. It seems unnecessary to provide more exact definitions here; on the essential points, what is meant will appear clearly from the context. I want only to point out that in this book the term aggression generally means behavior and reactions that inflict or have the purpose of inflicting injury on or discomfort to another individual. The term aggressive is closely bound up with this usage of the term aggression but also has a somewhat wider meaning. For a general background and more exact definitions, the reader is referred to an account given in another context (Olweus, 1973a).[4]

Finally, I shall comment briefly on one aspect of the choice of subjects; most such questions will be dealt with in the next chapter. The fact that the empirical investigations included only boys is due to a number of circumstances. Several instruments and research techniques that had already been tested in previous projects could be employed directly, or with slight modifi-

---

[4] In "Personality and Aggression" (Olweus, 1973a), an aggressive response (reaction) is defined as "any act or behavior that involves, might involve and/or to some extent can be considered as aiming at the infliction of injury or discomfort; also manifestations of inner reactions such as feelings or thoughts that can be considered to have such an aim are regarded as aggressive responses" (p. 270). In this context, I will also point out that I have little sympathy for theoretical formulations in which aggression is considered as an instinct, (e.g., Lorenz, 1966; Storr, 1968; Hartmann, Kris, & Loewenstein, 1949.

cations, on boys of the relevant ages. Much work in constructing and testing suitable research techniques would have been required in order to include girls as subjects. Moreover, there is generally more knowledge about aggression problems among boys than among girls: The results of empirical investigations on boys can thus be placed in a larger context of knowledge. This applies particularly to the effects of early parent-child relations. Finally, it can be presumed that whipping boy/bully problems are more common among boys and have more serious manifestations because of a stronger component of physical violence.

Thus the theory sketch in Figure 1 applies only to the boys in a class. Earlier investigations and the pilot studies also suggest that aggression variables and the problems to be taken up here can be validly studied for the age groups concerned when only the boys of a class take part in the investigation. Thus, from a research technical point of view, the negative effects of the omission of the girls should be trivial.

3

METHODS AND SUBJECTS–
OVERVIEW

As the theory sketch in Chapter 2 should have made clear, a number of different factors or groups of factors may be of significance for the appearance of whipping boy and/or bully problems in school. This makes it advisable to study the problems from many different angles. In this book, a more or less complete account will be given of five different investigations (comprising approximately 1,000 boys in all). These investigations differ somewhat in their starting points and main purposes, which has of course led to some variation in the planning of the studies. Certain general considerations, however, lay behind the design of the project as a whole. These strivings or goals are expressed below in the form of three guiding principles. They have been of particular importance for the design of the investigations on the Solna boys, and in the following analyses it is these studies that will be given most weight.

1. It is desirable to include several of the presumably significant factors or variables from each of the different sectors of the theory sketch. In the empirical investigations, data were collected on such things as (a) factors in the *school setting* that may be significant for or reflect the group climate (e.g., size of the school and the class, indications of the peer relations in the class, the attitude of the teachers to their profession); (b) *external characteristics* of the individual boys (e.g., height,

19

weight, deviations in appearance, dress, speech); (c) *psychological and behavior characteristics* (various tests and ratings as measures of different aspects of aggressiveness, degree of anxiety, self-esteem), as well as *characteristics reflecting the attitude or behavior of others* toward a boy (popularity according to sociometric choices, peer ratings of how often other boys fight with a particular boy, etc.). Data were also collected on (d) the social status of the family, some aspects of the parents' patterns of child rearing, and the boys' early childhood *(background and home conditions)*. For the most part, however, these last data have not yet been analyzed and will be presented in later reports.

2. It is desirable to obtain information or data from several different "informants" within a particular category (e.g., the boys in a class) as well as from informants from several different categories (e.g., boys, teachers, parents). It is obvious that a situation or problem may appear very different to different individuals, and this may, of course, occur for such a contentious phenomenon as mobbing. It therefore seemed important in these projects to attempt to obtain at least partly comparable data from "independent" informants. Accordingly, on many points, information will be found from teachers, peers, the "subjects" themselves, and in some cases from the subjects' mother *(different categories of assessors)*. Furthermore, in several of the investigations, two teachers (i.e., *assessors from the same category*) made assessments independently of each other, and in the peer ratings at least three boys from each class usually took part. This last procedure makes it possible to establish the degree of agreement between assessments of independent assessors within the same category, providing valuable information on the reliability of the assessments (interrater reliability).

3. It is desirable to study the problems by several different methods or techniques. This requirement is to some extent bound up with the previous one, and under certain conditions the different categories of informants may be regarded as different methods. What I want to stress here is that it is valuable to have some variation in the design of the research procedures or the instruments employed within a particular

sector or for a particular category of informants. Such a strategy may help to avoid irrelevant "method variance," that is, that systematic relationships arise only or mostly because the different research procedures contain the same or similar elements. For instance, several different types of procedures have been employed in studying the boys: a number of inventories, both of a conventional type and in the form of a special variant, the so-called Q sort; rating scales where the subjects are to place themselves or their peers along scales with (usually) 7 steps; sociometric techniques in which the subject has to select a given number of classmates with whom he would prefer to spend the breaks; projective methods with ambiguous stimulus material— which are usually assumed to measure less conscious sides of the personality.[1] These variations in research techniques also make it possible to study the problems on a broad basis and from several different angles.

These remarks should make it clear that the empirical data collected are of widely varying kinds. Generally, however, an attempt has been made to obtain information or data that fulfill the criteria of being both *relevant* and *quantifiable*. Quantifiability implies that the data can fairly easily be expressed in or converted to scores or numerical values. This makes it possible to employ conventional statistical methods in the analysis of data. Even though many of the data to be presented are of this kind, it should be pointed out that many "soft" data were also collected. These take the form of descriptive comments and informal hypotheses obtained primarily in connection with the interviews with the teachers. Some of these data, too, will be presented in a later chapter, with the object of exemplifying and highlighting the problems under study.

SUBJECT GROUPS AND PROCEDURES

General Design

After this survey of the general methodological background of the investigations, the next step is to describe the different

---

[1] In this book, however, the results from projective methods are given only limited attention, see p. 116.

subject groups and the procedures employed for each group. Even though some points will be treated in more detail in later sections, it is impossible within the scope of this book to provide a fully satisfactory account of the subject groups, methods, and data analyses. However, some analyses containing more detailed information will be presented in the professional journals of psychology.

As already stated, the research project involved five groups comprising approximately 1,000 boys in all. Four of these groups came from the sixth grade, age 12-14 years, and one came from the eighth grade, age 14-16 years. In this book, two of the groups (the second and third Solna investigations) will be referred to only on certain points, since a considerable part of the material for these groups has not yet been analyzed. Of the remaining three investigations, which dealt with boys from the sixth grade, the first Solna investigations will receive the most weight: This study was designed to cover systematically the different sectors of the whipping boy/bully problems. The two other investigations (the Stockholm groups) contain valuable information on certain sectors but are incomplete on others, since they were not planned primarily for studying the mobbing problem and its ramifications.

With one exception, the empirical investigations have been nonexperimental; that is, the data have been collected with the aid of tests and other techniques without arranging special conditions for one or more subgroups of subjects. In one investigation, however, an experimental procedure was used (different subgroups were shown either aggressive or non-aggressive feature films, and one subgroup was not shown any film at all). In this instance, mainly the data from the non-experimental part of the investigation (before the experimental manipulations) have been used.

A considerable number of the investigations were carried out in groups, with either the whole class or just the boys from the classroom. By means of the teachers' assessments of the boys, it was possible to pick out special subgroups, such as whipping boys and bullies, according to specified criteria. These *special groups* will be of particular interest in many of the following analyses.

For tests or other tasks carried out with one subject at a time, a room at the school could usually be obtained. In the individual investigations, other boys in the class in addition to the whipping boys or bullies always took part, in order to avoid drawing attention to certain categories of boys. In all investigations, the subjects were informed—in words suited to their ages—that their answers and the information they gave would be used only for research purposes.

Common Data

Certain procedures and variables have been used in chiefly the same form throughout the five investigations. Other procedures and variables have been employed, possibly with some modifications, in two or more investigations. Some are represented in only one investigation. A brief account of the design of the procedures that were employed in all five investigations follows. Where available, information about reliability and validity are reported in connection with the results for the technique in question.

Teachers' assessments were used in all the investigations in order to identify the boys in a class who were whipping boys or bullies. In a structured interview, the teacher was asked to consider whether he or she had one or more boys in the class who could be described as a whipping boy or bully according to specified criteria (see Chapter 4). In the same interview, the teacher was also asked to select the boys in the class who could be designated as well adjusted according to specified criteria. This category of boys was included in certain investigations as an interesting comparison group.

These assessments were always made by the main teacher (see footnote 3, p. 15), as it could be assumed he or she would know more about the class than the other teachers. In several of the investigations, however, information was also gained on each class from an additional teacher, the woodwork teacher as a rule. The selection of special groups was based mainly on these assessments made by the teachers. As will be seen later, independent ratings made by peers provide strong support for the adequacy of the teachers' assessments.

The criteria for whipping boys and bullies mentioned above were not so precisely formulated in the two Stockholm investigations as in the three Solna studies. In consequence, in the Stockholm investigations, the teachers' verbal comments on the boys selected have been given more weight in choosing the special groups. This fact is not likely to have led to noteworthy differences between the Stockholm and Solna investigations with regard to the composition and character of the special groups; the peer ratings provide strong support for this view. However, due to this circumstance, the Stockholm groups are less useful as a basis for determining the relative frequency of the whipping boy/bully problem.

Peer ratings were also used in all the investigations as a method of obtaining information about typical behavior by the boys and about certain aspects of the peer relations in a class. A boy selected to make peer ratings was asked to place cards containing the names of all his classmates on a piece of cardboard below squares representing different degrees of the variable in question. The variable dealing with physical aggression, for example, was worded as follows:

He starts fights with other boys at school.

1	2	3	4	5	6	7
very seldom	seldom	rather seldom	some-times	rather often	often	very often

The rater placed one card at a time beneath the box best suited to the boy concerned. Each boy thus received a score of 1-7. (This variable will be called Start Fights.)

In addition to the variable just given, the following 7-point variables occurred most frequently: "Other boys at school start fights and are rough with him and tease him" (Aggression Target); "When a teacher criticizes him, he tends to answer back and protest" (Verbal Protest); "He is liked by none or almost none of the boys in the class—all the boys in the class" (Popularity); He teases other boys at school" (possibly more indirect aggression against other boys, called Tease).

As a rule, from three to five boys were randomly selected from each class, and they independently carried out the peer ratings for all the variables. The average of the ratings on a particular variable was used as the subject's score for that variable.

The frequent use of peer ratings in my projects has given me comprehensive experience in this technique of collecting information. In sum, the experience has been predominantly positive, in terms of interrater agreement, validity, stability over time, and theoretical relevance (see, e.g., Olweus 1969, 1973a, 1975).

THE FIRST SOLNA INVESTIGATION

The total investigation involved all the boys in the sixth grade at Solna, 299 in all. The approximately 300 girls in this grade also participated to some degree (in the inventory "Our Class" and sociometric choices, see below), but except for the sociometric choices, the answers from the girls have not yet been analyzed. The boys were distributed over 26 classes, of which 4 were so-called special classes (two reading and two remedial classes). The 26 classes belonged to 11 different schools. No exact information as to age was collected, but several earlier investigations have shown that the ages for the sixth grade vary from 12 to 14, with a median age of 13 in the spring term. From this population, three special groups were selected, comprised of 21 whipping boys, 21 bullies, and 22 well-adjusted boys. For some of the analyses, a control group consisting of 60 randomly chosen boys was used.

On page 26 is a résumé of the techniques and variables that have been more fully analyzed for the total group and the special groups. The heading "Only for the special groups" indicates that the data or variables given refer only to those groups. The presentation of the material corresponds with the sector divisions used in the theory sketch.

Sector A—Factors in the school setting that can be
assumed to be of significance for or reflect the
group climate, etc.

Number of pupils in the school, number of pupils in the
class, number of boys in the class.
Interview with teachers on peer relations in the class, general
attitude of the class to schoolwork, teachers' general
evaluation of the class, and teachers' satisfaction with
their profession.
The inventory "Our Class" (modified after Johannesson,
1966), whose aim is to provide information (from the
boys) on peer relations in the class, general attitude to
schoolwork, and attitude to teachers.
Peer ratings on certain variables that can be assumed to
reflect peer relations in the class (Start Fights, Tease,
Aggression Target).

Sector B—External, Physical Characteristics

Only for the special groups

Teachers' assessments of possible deviations in appearance,
dress, speech, physical strength, etc. (checklist).
Height, weight.

Sector C—Psychological characteristics, behavior characteristics, and characteristics reflecting the attitude
or behavior of others toward an individual

Teachers' assessments of the boys according to the criteria
for whipping boys, bullies, and well-adjusted boys.
Peer ratings on five variables (Start Fights, Aggression Target,
Verbal Protest, Popularity, Tease).
Sociometric choices with regard to the boys (choices made
by both boys and girls in the class.

Only for the special groups

Grades.
Teachers' assessments of "ability to profit from instruction."
Q sort, a special questionnaire technique in which the
subject has to decide, according to certain rules, how

well each of a number of statements fits him. In this Q sort, 57 items were included covering, among other areas, aggression and violence, anxiety, identification, self-esteem, and contact with parents. (The Q sort was individually administered.)

The same Q sort as above but filled out by the mothers about their sons. Thus, by means of the Q sort, the mothers gave a psychological description of their boys.

Teachers' assessments or free descriptions of the boys in connection with the interviews.

Sector D—Background and home conditions

Only for the special groups

Some social data about the family: age, work, and education of parents (social groups).

Follow-Up of First Solna Group

Slightly more than a year after the interview in the sixth grade, the boys' main teachers and in some cases also their gymnastics teachers were interviewed again. The boys had now advanced to a more senior stage and 18 of the 26 classes had moved into other school buildings. Of the 26 classes, 24 had new main teachers. None of the new teachers knew anything about the investigation undertaken the previous year. Consequently, it was possible to study in a meaningful way questions concerning the stability of whipping boy/bully problems. To what extent would the new teachers choose the same boys as whipping boys or bullies as those selected in the sixth grade? What factors could be assumed to be responsible if marked changes had taken place? How would the new teachers assess the peer relations in the class as compared with the assessments of the previous year? The follow-up in the seventh grade involved 293 boys. In the period between the first and second investigations, 13 boys had moved from Solna, 2 had died, and 9 had moved to Solna. The 26 classes, still including 4 special classes, were distributed among 7 schools.

In grade 7, peer ratings on two variables (Start Fights and

Aggression Target) were carried out for 8 of the 26 classes (see Chapter 5). Furthermore, in grade 9, three years after the first rating occasion, follow-up ratings on four variables (Start Fights, Verbal Protest, Aggression Target, and Popularity) were obtained for 18 classes, comprising a total of 201 boys (see Chapter 7). By means of these data, it was possible to measure the stability of the peer relations as reflected by these variables over both a 1-year and a 3-year interval. Since there had been changes in schools, teachers, and peer group composition, the data also permitted a study of the influence of variations in certain factors in the school setting.

The follow-up investigations on the first Solna group were limited to questions of this kind (Sector A and Sector C), and the material used to shed light on them was drawn mainly from interviews with the teachers and from peer ratings.

THE FIRST STOCKHOLM INVESTIGATION

Participants in this investigation were 113 boys from 10 classes in the sixth grade. These classes were from three schools in the central and southern areas of Stockholm. The chief purpose of the investigation was to construct and test techniques for the study of various aggression dimensions. Some of the material will be briefly reported since it serves as an independent test of points treated more exhaustively in the first Solna investigation: (1) the agreement between independent teacher assessments—selection of whipping boys and bullies in this material was made by two teachers for each class, the main teacher and the woodwork teacher; (2) the correspondence between teacher assessments and peer ratings—peer ratings were made here on the five variables mentioned earlier.

In addition, a special projective method known as the Defence Mechanism Test, constructed by Kragh (1960, 1969) was used in this investigation. Since adequate presentation of the method is beyond the scope of this book, only a summary statement of the main results will be given (see footnote 5, p. 116). All boys in the subject group were tested (individually) by this method, with particular interest centered on three special groups, consisting of 10 whipping boys, 10 bullies, and 15 well-adjusted boys, selected on the basis of the teachers' assessments.

Sector C

Teachers' assessments of the boys according to the criteria for whipping boys, bullies, and well-adjusted boys (in addition, free verbal descriptions of the boys selected).
Peer assessments on the five variables.
Defence Mechanism Test.

THE SECOND STOCKHOLM INVESTIGATION

Participants in this investigation were 142 boys from 12 sixth-grade classes distributed over six schools in east, central, and southern Stockholm. The main object of this investigation was to study possible effects of viewing an aggression-saturated feature film. Before the total group was divided into experimental subgroups, however, all the boys were tested with the same procedures and under the same conditions. In addition, teachers' assessments and peer ratings were collected with regard to the boys' usual behavior.

Partial results from this investigation are reported here, with the main object of contributing to the psychological picture of the whipping boys and bullies. The special groups studied consist of 10 whipping boys, 11 bullies, and a control group of 60 boys selected at random from the rest of the subjects.

Sector C

Teachers' assessments of the boys according to the criteria for whipping boys, bullies, and well-adjusted boys (in addition, free verbal descriptions of the boys selected).
Peer ratings on four variables.
A form containing 30 statements designed to measure the boys' attitudes toward themselves (e.g., anxiety), their situation (e.g., contact with parents), and schoolwork. The form is referred to as the self-evaluation form in the following.

A semantic differential consisting of 15 adjective pairs such as: anxious—bold, quick—slow, strong—weak. This technique was also designed to reflect, in a slightly different way, the boys' self-evaluation—to what degree they had a positive or negative attitude toward themselves.

The form Aggressive Attitude, containing 17 statements from four different areas: positive attitude toward physical violence, being "well brought up," aggression against adults, and negative attitude to deviants.

THE SECOND AND THIRD
SOLNA INVESTIGATIONS

Two more investigations used boys from Solna. One involved 19 out of 27 classes in the sixth grade, 217 boys in all—approximately 75% of the boys in the grade. The third Solna investigation consisted of a parallel selection from the eighth grade: 18 out of 26 classes, 215 boys in all; representing approximately 75% of the boys in the grade.

A great many data were collected on both these subject groups, partly by methods used earlier and partly by new methods. Among the new methods were extensive parent interviews and yet another projective instrument, the Holzman Inkblot Technique. As with the first Solna investigation, these two Solna investigations provide opportunities for studying variables in all sectors of the theory sketch. In particular, the parent interviews are expected to supply increased knowledge about Sector D—the boys' background and home conditions.

As already stated, a considerable part of this material has not yet been analyzed. The information will be employed here in the following ways: (1) To establish, on the basis of the teachers' assessments, the relative occurrence of whipping boys and bullies in the respective grades (Chapter 4). (2) In analyses of possible deviations in appearance and "ability to profit from instruction" (Sectors B and C, Chapters 6 and 7). Here, too, teachers' assessments will be employed, but in this case only for boys in the sixth grade. (3) To provide an independent test of the Q sort results obtained in the first Solna investigation

(Sector C, Chapter 7). The boys in the second Solna investigation were given the 57 items from the Q sort in the format of a conventional inventory. The data analyses were mainly based on a group of 15 whipping boys, a group of 17 bullies, and a control group of 60 boys randomly selected from the rest of the boys.

METHODS OF DATA ANALYSIS

As a rule, the data have been analyzed by conventional statistical methods, such as one-way analysis of variance (F and t tests, χ^2, product-moment correlation, and phi correlation). For descriptions of these techniques, the reader is referred to general textbooks in psychological statistics, such as Hays (1973), McNemar (1969), and Winer (1971).

Two-tailed tests of significance have generally been used in spite of the fact that one-tailed tests would be defensible in many cases. Usually, results with a probability value (p value) of .05 or less have been regarded as significant or statistically reliable. However, in the analyses of individual statements in Chapter 7, p values as large as .10 have been reported and considered. For these statements, three independent sets of data were usually available.

As recommended in several recent presentations of psychological statistics (e.g., Cohen, 1965; Hays, 1973), a measure of the strength of the relationship has often been included as a complement to the significance test. For the most part, the "unbiased" correlation ratio, *epsilon* has been used in addition to the F test in analysis of variance (Cohen, 1965). The epsilon coefficient is closely related to the "universal" correlation measure *eta* and to Hays's *omega*. It should be noted that epsilon coefficients derived from *different* investigations are not always directly comparable. The same is true of eta and omega coefficients.

In some of the analyses, a control group, to be compared with the whipping boy and bully groups, was formed by random selection from the remainder of the boys in the relevant subject group. There are statistical reasons for not using *all* the remaining boys as a comparison group. If the number of individuals in the statistical analyses is large, significant results may easily be obtained even with small differences or weak relationships in the population. By employing a comparison group of moderate size (e.g., 40–60 boys), the interpretation of results is limited to the more pronounced differences or relationships—which can be discovered with a reasonable number of subjects. By this means, the risks of overinterpreting the results are reduced.

Another safeguard against these risks is that the majority of the data analyses of the same or similar variables could be carried out on different, independent groups of subjects. Of course, similar findings in repeated analyses on different groups—replications—increase considerably the trustworthiness of the results obtained.

As already indicated, some more descriptive, nonstatistical analyses will also be reported (Chapter 7).

DISPOSITION OF THE FOLLOWING REPORT

Chapter 4 first analyzes some characteristics of the teachers' assessments of the boys and then estimates how frequent whipping boy and bully problems are. This leads, in Chapter 5, to the question of possible links between relative frequency of problems in a class and various factors in the school setting (Sector A). Chapter 6 deals primarily with the problem of external deviations, that is, factors in Sector B. In Chapter 7, an analysis of psychological characteristics of whipping boys and bullies (Sector C) is undertaken, and certain data about the social background (Sector D) are studied. The results obtained form the basis of an account of the entire complex of whipping boy/bully problems in Chapter 8. Finally, Chapter 9 contains a discussion of the goals of a program of change and a proposal for such a program.

4

INCIDENCE OF WHIPPING BOY/ BULLY PROBLEMS

Do whipping boy/bully problems really exist in our schools? Or are the occasional instances of persecution and bullying that are reported in the press just exaggerations and distortions? Are there boys in our schools who can truthfully be described as either typical whipping boys or bullies? Isn't it rather that sometimes one boy, sometimes another, becomes the object of his classmates' irritation and dislike? Is it really possible in our well-controlled school settings that certain boys should often and over long periods of time be exposed to aggression from others or should themselves oppress others?

DEFINITIONS OF WHIPPING BOY AND BULLY

To find answers to these and other related questions, structured interviews with the main teachers of the classes investigated were used. It could be expected that these teachers had a sound knowledge of the relations in the class and also of the individual boys; as a rule the main teacher had had the class throughout the whole of the middle stage, that is, almost 3 years for the boys in the sixth grade, and had been together with them many hours during the week, usually not less than 20 periods.

Of course, the answers given at an interview depend to a great degree on the wording of the questions asked. Accordingly, much time and effort were spent on making sure that the questions were as clear as possible, and on essential points precisely the same wording was used by the interviewer in each interview. The teachers' answers were entered on special forms or for questions about external deviations, were crossed off on a checklist. The order in which the various items in the interview were taken up was fixed, and the same interviewer interviewed all the teachers in a particular investigation. Three of the interviewers were qualified psychologists and the fourth nearly qualified.[1]

The teachers were briefly informed by letter of the general background and purpose of the investigation. On meeting the teacher, the interviewer first referred to the information in this letter and then asked the teacher to consider whether there were one or more boys in the class who in the teacher's opinion were pronounced whipping boys. At this point, the interviewer provided the following specification: "A *pronounced whipping boy* is a boy who for a fairly long time has been and still is exposed to aggression from others; that is, boys or possibly girls from his own class or maybe from other classes often pick fights and are rough with him or tease and ridicule him." Through further questions, the teacher was asked to give a general description of what he or she thought the boy in question was like, how the boy reacted when picked on by others, whether one or several of the others picked on him, and approximately how long he had been a whipping boy.

It should be noted that according to the definition given above, the whipping boy is exposed to some form of active aggression on the part of other pupils; he is not just the object of indifference, unpopularity, or other more passive expressions of dislike. The definition also stresses that the behavior must have occurred over quite some time; this was insisted on in

---

[1] The same female interviewers were used in the first Solna investigation and in the follow-up study a year later. One female interviewer did all the interviewing in the later Solna investigations. In the Stockholm investigations, both the interviewers were men.

order to exclude boys who had been the target of aggression for only a short period. The teacher who was interviewed was given the opportunity to read the definition, and in the later Solna investigations received a written statement of it. (The same was done for the bullies and well-adjusted boys.)

After picking out and describing possible pronounced whipping boys, the teacher had to consider whether there were boys in the class who might be classified as bullies. The definition of a bully was as follows: "A *bully* is a boy who fairly often oppresses or harasses somebody else; the target may be boys or girls, the harassment physical or mental." This wording was intended to designate pronounced bullies, but the word "pronounced" was not used in the definition given to the teachers. The same or similar additional questions as those asked about whipping boys were asked about bullies.

After this, the teacher was requested to consider whether there were boys in the class who were *less pronounced whipping boys or bullies*, that is, boys who showed only tendencies toward being one or the other. The reason for including this less strongly worded question was that it could be assumed that at least some of the teachers would find it difficult to admit that pronounced whipping boys or bullies were to be found in their classes.

A fourth main question asked the teacher to think about whether any of the boys mentioned, or other boys in the class, showed signs of *fluctuating between being whipping boy and bully*. Insofar as this occurred at all, the teacher had as a rule already made the point in connection with some of the earlier questions.

The fifth main question aimed at picking out the (three) *best-adjusted boys* in the class. The interviewer pointed out that it is not easy to define what is meant by "well-adjusted" boys, but that in this context it meant "boys who by and large are content with life, self-confident, get on well with boys and adults, and show good ability to cooperate with others." The interviewer emphasized that naturally one and the same boy seldom had all these qualities but that these qualities could help the teacher to understand what we were looking for. The central aim in getting assessments of "good adjustment" was to find, for purposes of comparison, a group of boys whom the teacher regarded as secure, harmonious, and generally satisfied under existing conditions. It should perhaps be noted that no demands for intelligence or for being clever at school were included in the definition. In some of the analyses, the well-adjusted groups are of minor interest.

After these main questions, the teacher was asked to consider, in turn, all the boys mentioned in the answers so far and to indicate whether the boy was unusual or deviating in appearance, dress, or manner when compared with boys in general. The interview, which usually lasted about an hour, closed with four questions on the teacher's opinion of the class in certain respects and on the teacher's attitude to the teaching profession. This part of the interview material is dealt with in Chapters 5 and 6.

AGREEMENT BETWEEN
INDEPENDENT TEACHER ASSESSMENTS

Before figures dealing with the frequency of whipping boy/bully problems are presented, the question of agreement between independent teacher assessments will be considered. In spite of the definitions offered, it is still possible that a teacher would make selections according to his or her own criteria and that another teacher would judge the same boys quite differently. This might depend on various circumstances, for instance, the second teacher to some extent might use different criteria and/or the boys' behavior might be different toward this teacher. There are obvious grounds for attempting to establish whether two teachers having the same class arrive at approximately the same assessments or whether there is hardly more than chance agreement.

Method and Results

The first Solna and the first Stockholm investigations will be employed to throw light on this question. In the Solna investigation, 26 main teachers and 12 woodwork teachers took part. The woodwork teachers taught more than one class, usually two or three classes of the relevant age group. Some circumstances that might be expected to reduce the woodwork teachers' degree of agreement with the main teachers should be mentioned. The woodwork teachers had taught their respective classes for a much shorter period than the main teachers, usually for not more than a school year, and in addition for not more than two hours a week. The woodwork teachers must therefore be regarded generally as having less knowledge about the boys than the main teachers (several woodwork teachers also pointed this out). On the other hand, the form of work and the general intercourse are freer and more flexible in the handicrafts room, and these conditions make for good opportunities for observing the boys' behavior toward each other.

Table 1 shows the degree of agreement between the 26 main teachers' and the 12 woodwork teachers' assessments of 294

TABLE 1

Agreement in Assessments Made by
Main Teachers and Woodwork Teachers, Grade 6

		Woodwork teachers ($n = 12$)			No. of boys
		+	0	−	
	+	18	18	0	36
Main teachers ($n = 26$)	0	14	215	5	234
	−	0	12	12	24
Total		32	245	17	294

+ Assessed as pronounced bully or less pronounced bully (tendency).
− Assessed as pronounced whipping boy or less pronounced whipping boy (tendency).
0 Not mentioned in category + or −.

$\chi^2 = 157.05$ $df = 4$
$p < .0001$
$C = .59$ $C_{.05} = .18$
        $C_{max} = .82$

Percentage agreement $= \dfrac{245}{294} = 83\%$

boys (5 boys were assessed by only 1 teacher). The material is divided into three categories: pronounced bully or less pronounced bully (+), pronounced whipping boy or less pronounced whipping boy (−), those not mentioned in either of the preceding categories (0). The few boys considered to fluctuate between whipping boy and bully have been placed under their dominating category.

The question of whether there was more than a chance relationship between the assessments of the main and woodwork teachers was tested statistically with the aid of χ^2. The value of χ^2 was 157.05 and the probability of obtaining such a high value as a result of chance is less than .0001; that is, the relationship was statistically very significant. As a measure of the strength of the relationship, the contingency coefficient C was used and for this table, $C = .59$. It should be noted that in a 3 × 3 table the maximum value C can reach is .82 and that a value of .18 is sufficient for C to be significantly different from 0, for the actual number of individuals and degrees of freedom.

The degree of agreement can also be expressed as a percentage. In Table 1, the main and woodwork teachers' assessments agreed for 245 of the 294 boys; that is, there was 83% agreement.

In setting up tables of this type, it is usually possible, as regards a small part of the material, to place individuals in more than one category: in this case, for example, the boys whom one or both teachers had assessed as fluctuating between whipping boy and bully. Furthermore, two classes about which the woodwork teacher declared himself very uncertain could have been excluded from the statistical analyses. Calculations based on such slightly modified tables gave results that on the whole corresponded with the results in Table 1: The C value varied between .53 and .64, all highly significant, with agreement between 82 and 87%.

The results for the 113 boys in the first Stockholm investigation will also be presented. As mentioned, the whipping boy and bully definitions were not so strictly formulated in this investigation. Even so, a contingency coefficient of .62 was obtained for agreement between the main and woodwork teachers' assessments, $p < .0001$.

Comments

The results of the above analyses show that there was a substantial degree of agreement between main and woodwork teachers when assessing, independently, whether a boy was a whipping boy or a bully or neither. This was true of both the Solna and the Stockholm investigations. Expressed somewhat differently, the results thus imply that the boys were distinguished by certain systematic relations to their peers and that these relations were to a considerable degree assessed in the same way by different teachers, in spite of differences in their knowledge of the boys and differences in the situations on which the assessments were based.

Even though there was substantial interteacher agreement, I have chosen, in the frequency analyses and in the selection of special groups, to put most weight on the assessments made by the main teachers since they generally could be regarded as having a more thorough knowledge of the boys.

AGREEMENT BETWEEN
INDEPENDENT TEACHER ASSESSMENTS,
GRADES 6 AND 7

The definition of a pronounced whipping boy presented to the teachers stipulated that the behavior must have continued for a fairly long time. The teachers also provided information on this point, and it turned out that many boys had been whipping boys or bullies for several years. In spite of this, it might be thought that relatively rapid changes would occur and that no great degree of stability in the relations would be found, in particular if there were a change of schools (as occurred to 18 out of the 26 classes in the transition from grade 6 to grade 7) and teachers (24 of the 26 classes got new teachers). The follow-up study of the boys in the first Solna investigation provided an opportunity to throw light on these questions. Only certain aspects of the follow-up will be dealt with here; other aspects will be discussed later.

Method and Results

As mentioned in Chapter 3, the main teachers for the seventh grade were also interviewed personally, about a year after the first teacher interviews were completed. For 10 of the 26 classes—especially those in which it could be assumed that the main teacher did not know the class well—the gymnastics teacher was also interviewed. Because of the way woodwork classes were arranged in the seventh grade, it was considered more helpful to interview the gymnastics teachers rather than the woodwork teachers.

On all essential points, the interviews were carried out in the same way as in the previous year. In addition, thorough inquiries were made as to whether the teachers knew anything about the earlier investigation. As mentioned, two teachers had accompanied their classes to the seventh grade and thus had been interviewed in the first investigation. All the other teachers stated that they knew nothing at all about the investigation in the sixth grade. The results of the analyses below remain very nearly the same, if the two teachers interviewed earlier are excluded.

The degree of agreement between the teacher assessments in the sixth and seventh grades can be calculated in several slightly different ways. Table 2 is based on the assessments given by the main teachers for the sixth grade, excluding three boys who received only woodwork teachers' assessments. For the seventh grade, the main teachers' and/or the gymnastics teachers' assessments were employed. In using this procedure, an attempt was made to base the calculations on the most reliable information available, the apparent reliability of the assessments being judged from the teachers' verbal descriptions and from their knowledge of the class.

As Table 2 reveals, there was a very significant relationship between the different assessments in the two grades. The contingency coefficient was .63, and the percentage agreement was 84%. In all, 286 boys were assessed in both grades.

If only the main teachers' assessments are taken into account, a somewhat lower χ^2 value is reached, 140.27, $p <$ .0001, and the contingency coefficient becomes .57. The percentage agreement is 82%.

Table 2 shows that 24 out of the 35 boys picked out as pronounced or less pronounced bullies in grade 6 were selected as belonging to the same category 1 year later. That is, 69% of the sixth-grade bullies were assessed by independent teachers to be bullies also in grade 7. In comparison, the percentage of bullies for the group as a whole was 12% (34 out of 286) in grade 7. When the calculations were restricted to those boys who were assessed as pronounced bullies in grade 6, it was found that 81% of these boys were selected as pronounced or less pronounced bullies in grade 7.

For the whipping boys, the corresponding percentage values were 59% (16 out of 27) and 69%. The second value was obtained when the analyses were confined to the pronounced whipping boys from grade 6.

TABLE 2

Agreement in Assessments Made by
Main Teachers in Grades 6 and 7

		Grade 7			No. of boys
		+	0	−	
	+	24	9	2	35
Grade 6	0	9	200	15	224
	−	1	10	16	27
Total		34	219	33	286

+ Assessed as pronounced bully or less pronounced bully (tendency).
− Assessed as pronounced whipping boy or less pronounced whipping boy (tendency).
0 Not mentioned in category + or −.

$\chi^2 = 188.72$ $df = 4$
$p < .0001$
$C = .63$ $C_{.05} = .18$
          $C_{max} = .82$

Percentage agreement $= \dfrac{240}{286} = 84\%$

Comments

The above analyses indicate that to a large extent the same boys were assessed as whipping boys and bullies, respectively, on the two assessment occasions separated by a 1-year interval.

The degree of agreement between the assessments for the sixth and seventh grades was actually as great as or greater than the agreement between the main and woodwork teachers in their assessments in grade 6 (Table 1). It should also be stressed that probably some "real" whipping boys and bullies in the seventh grade remained "undiscovered," since the new teachers had not yet acquired a thorough knowledge of the relations in the class: They had had the classes for less than a school year and, moreover, only taught them for a few periods, an average of 5–6 hours, per week. The assessments in the seventh grade thus showed a striking agreement with the corresponding assessments in the sixth grade—and this in spite of the fact that the boys had new teachers, were mostly at new schools, and were a year older. Naturally, some changes had occurred, but the predominating impression from the analyses is of stable or very stable relationships: *To be a whipping boy or a bully is obviously something that may extend over long periods of time.*

PEER RATINGS OF WHIPPING BOYS AND BULLIES

The conclusions formulated in the last sections were founded on the teachers' assessments. It is conceivable, though it seems unlikely in view of the analyses above, that the teachers had their own stereotyped ideas about whipping boys and bullies and that their judgments had very little to do with the actual relations between the boys concerned. The relations between the boys might look different seen through the eyes of the boys. The peer ratings made by the boys can be used to shed light on this question. This point concerns one aspect of the *validity* of the teachers' assessments, that is, whether they in fact measure what they are intended to measure.

Method and Results

As stated in Chapter 3, a selection of boys in each class made peer ratings on five variables, three concerning aggressive behavior toward others (Start Fights, Verbal Protest, Tease), one on aggressive behavior by other boys (Aggression Target) and one on popularity among the boys in the class (Popularity). On some of these variables, it is perhaps not quite obvious what should be expected in the way of differences or lack of differences among the groups, but provided the teachers' assessments were valid, at least the following relations should hold: The bullies should have higher values than a randomly selected control group (and probably also than the whipping boys) on the variable Start Fights; the whipping boys should have higher values than a control group (and probably also than the bullies) on the variable Aggression Target; it would be reasonable for the whipping boys to have lower values than a control group on the variable Popularity. On other points, various results may be conjectured, depending on one's views on the whole complex of problems. This does not imply, however, that all result patterns would be equally meaningful.

One important point about the peer ratings should be emphasized: The boys made their assessments without the whipping boy/bully problem being mentioned to them. Their task was simply to assess the other boys in the class in the respects concerned. It is thus very unlikely that possible preconceived opinions on whipping boys and bullies affected their judgments. Table 3 and Figure 2 show the chief results of the peer ratings in the first Solna investigation. The groups attracting most interest in the present context are: (1) a group of 21 whipping boys selected primarily on the basis of the main teachers' assessments and, in a few cases, the woodwork teachers' assessments only; this special group represents the most marked whipping boys in the material; (2) a group of 21 bullies, chiefly selected on the basis of the main teachers' assessments and, in one case, the woodwork teacher's assessment; this group comprised the most marked bullies; (3) a control group consisting of 60 boys chosen at random from the total subject groups after the 42 boys in groups 1 and 2 had been withdrawn. It may be mentioned that the mean values for the control group on the variables concerned came out very close to the means for the total subject group including whipping boys and bullies.

It is evident from Table 3 and Figure 2 that very marked differences existed among the groups. As expected, the bullies began fights far more often than the boys in the control group, $p < .0001$, and the whipping boys, $p < .0001$, but, in addition,

TABLE 3

Mean Values, F values,
and Epsilon Coefficients for Peer Ratings

Variable	Mean values	F	Epsilon
Start Fights	Wh = 2.27 B = 4.39 C = 2.47 t $test^a$: B > C = Wh	24.30 $p < .0001$	.56
Verbal Protest	Wh = 2.30 B = 5.14 C = 3.14 t test: B > C > Wh	32.39 $p < .0001$	.62
Tease	Wh = 2.49 B = 5.02 C = 3.03 t test: B > C = Wh	30.14 $p < .0001$	.60
Aggression Target	Wh = 4.58 B = 2.43 C = 2.63 t test: Wh > C = B	22.97 $p < .0001$	.55
Popularity	Wh = 2.56 B = 3.68 C = 3.85 t test: Wh < B = C	9.15 $p < .0001$	.37

Wh = Whipping boys ($n = 21$).
B = Bullies ($n = 21$).
C = Control group ($n = 60$).

^{a}Two-tailed t tests and a .05 significance level were used.

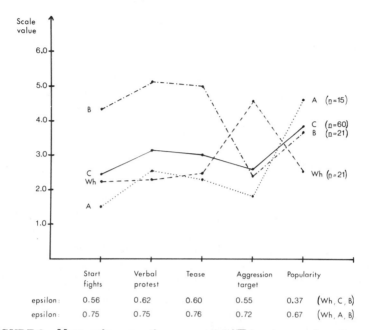

FIGURE 2. Mean values on the peer rating dimensions and epsilon coefficients for comparisons between whipping boys (Wh), control boys (C), and bullies (B) and whipping boys (Wh), well-adjusted boys (A), and bullies (B) in the first Solna investigation. For significance at the .05 level, an epsilon value of .24 is required in the Wh, C, and B comparison. The corresponding value in the Wh, A, and B comparison is .31.

the bullies had much higher values on the two other aggression variables, $p < .0001$ in relation to the control group. The whipping boys showed the expected high values on the variable Aggression Target, $p = .0001$ in relation to the control group, and were also clearly less popular with their classmates than the control boys, $p < .0005$. In addition, the whipping boys showed lower mean values on all three variables for aggressive behavior, and two of these differences were significant or almost significant, for the variables Verbal protest, $p < .01$, and Tease, $p = .06$.

As appears from the epsilon coefficients, for most variables the relationships were of considerable strength, in comparison with what is common in psychological investigations of this character: A considerable part of the total variation in the peer ratings was thus associated with or could be predicted from the teachers' classification of the boys as whipping boys (Wh), bullies (B), or control boys (i.e., those not mentioned as whipping boys or bullies). The epsilon coefficients were even higher in the comparisons between the whipping boys, bullies, and the well-adjusted boys (A),[2] as is evident from the values in Figure 2. The figure also shows that the well-adjusted boys were clearly more popular than the other groups, $p < .01$ in relation to the control group.

Examination of the peer ratings for the two Stockholm investigations—with Wh, A, and B groups and Wh, C, and B groups selected on the basis of teacher assessments—revealed in all essentials the same picture as described for the Solna investigation. As an example, the F values for the Wh, A, and B groups for the three perhaps especially interesting variables Start Fights, Aggression Target, and Popularity were 7.61, $p < .005$ ($df = 2, 32$); 17.47, $p < .0001$; and 16.37, $p < .0001$. The corresponding epsilon coefficients were .54, .71, and .70. For significance at the .05 level, an epsilon value of .35 is needed.

Comments

The analyses reported in the last section actually deal with characteristics in Sector C of the theory sketch. I shall discuss the results in connection with the other variables of this type in Chapter 7 and will here take up only a few special points.

In the first place, it can be noted that the analyses of the peer ratings in three different investigations gave essentially concordant results. Among other things, the bullies were judged to be considerably more aggressive than average; the whipping boys were rated as less popular than boys in general and were more often the target of other boys' aggression. The results for

---

[2] The well-adjusted group consisted of boys selected on the basis of the main teachers' and the woodwork teachers' assessments, with the exception of boys in the four special classes. The well-adjusted group comprises 22 boys in the following analyses. That there are only 15 boys in the present context is due to the fact that 7 boys were included in the randomly selected control group.

the other variables also formed quite meaningful patterns. The well-adjusted boys were assessed as nonaggressive and very popular. It is noteworthy that the relationships between the teachers' classification of the boys and the peer ratings were quite strong. The results can thus be interpreted as providing very strong support for the validity of the teachers' assessments. Obviously, there was marked agreement between the teachers' assessments and the boys' ratings on variables that can be expected to have a close connection with whipping boy/bully relations.

INCIDENCE OF WHIPPING BOYS AND BULLIES

As mentioned earlier, the assessments made by the main teachers are the most adequate basis for frequency analyses. Table 4 shows the relative frequencies for the different categories in four subject groups: The first Solna investigation in grade 6, the follow-up study of the same boys in grade 7 (with

TABLE 4

Whipping Boys and Bullies
According to Main Teachers' Assessments

Category	Solna I Grade 6	Solna I Grade 7	Solna II Grade 6	Solna III Grade 8
Pronounced whipping boy	4.3%	3.7%	7.4%	7.4%
Less pronounced whipping boy	4.3%	6.8%	7.8%	6.1%
Not mentioned	79.0%	79.4%	74.7%	79.0%
Less pronounced bully	6.4%	6.4%	5.5%	1.9%
Pronounced bully	6.0%	3.7%	4.6%	5.6%
Pronounced whipping boy & bully	10.3%	7.4%	12.0%	13.0%
No. of boys	299	295	217[a]	215[a]

[a]Approximately 75% of boys in grade.

new teachers), and the last two Solna investigations, in grades 6 and 8. In these last investigations, the subject groups comprised approximately 75% of the total number of boys in the respective grade. Since the boys in all three special classes[3] in each grade were included in these two subject groups, the percentages for whipping boys and bullies given in the last two columns are likely to be somewhat too high. For, as will appear shortly, the percentage of whipping boys and bullies was higher in special classes than in ordinary classes, which thus can lead to somewhat "inflated" values for the subject groups investigated as compared with the grade as a whole. Approximate calculations for the whole grades suggest, however, that the differences in all likelihood are small, about .5-1% per category.

As regards the somewhat lower percentages for pronounced whipping boys and bullies in grade 7 as compared with the assessments for largely the same boys 1 year earlier, it should be kept in mind that the assessments in the later grade were carried out by teachers who had had the boys for less than a school year. This fact may have contributed to a somewhat restrictive use of the more extreme categories ("pronounced").

Allowing for circumstances of this kind, the predominating impression of Table 4 is that the results for the different subject groups show substantial agreement. Approximately 4-6% of the boys in the grade were pronounced whipping boys, and the percentage of pronounced bullies was roughly the same. The combined percentage of pronounced whipping boys and bullies was close to 10%. If the less pronounced whipping boys and bullies (tendency) are also included, a considerably higher value is reached, approximately 20%.

Grade 8 had a relatively low percentage of less pronounced bullies, but in the pronounced categories the values were at least as high as for grade 6. A reduction of the relative frequencies from grade 6 to grade 8 can thus hardly be noticed. It is possible, however, that the problems manifest themselves in a

---

[3] A special class consists of children who for one reason or another have difficulties in following the ordinary teaching or in adapting themselves to the activities in the school. Ordinary classes are those that are not special classes.

slightly different way in higher grades, since it is known from other investigations that use of physical violence tends to decrease with increasing age.

The distribution between the classes in the first Solna investigation will be studied more closely in the next chapter, but it may be stated immediately that the different classes showed substantial variations in the frequency of whipping boys and bullies. Of the 26 classes, 6 entirely lacked pronounced whipping boys and/or less pronounced whipping boys according to the teachers' assessments. Six classes lacked pronounced bullies or less pronounced bullies. In other classes, as many as 5 or 6 of the boys were judged to be whipping boys or bullies (including the ordinary classes).

Not unexpectedly, the special classes showed higher percentage averages than ordinary classes. Whereas the average percentage of pronounced whipping boys among boys in the ordinary classes amounted to 6%, it was 18% in the four special classes. The corresponding values for pronounced bullies were 7% and 18%.

It is also of interest to attempt to estimate how large a percentage of boys in the four groups fluctuated between being whipping boys and bullies. On the average, barely 10% of the boys assessed by one or another of the teachers as whipping boys (including less pronounced) were reported to be whipping boys on some occasions and bullies on others. A closer analysis revealed, however, that a large number of these boys quite decidedly belonged to one category or the other. A reasonable estimate would be that only 3-7% of the whipping boys/bullies could be considered as "genuine fluctuators." For some of these boys, high values were found in the peer ratings on both of the variables Aggression Target and Start Fights.

Comments

On the basis of the above analyses, approximately 10% of the boys in the grades investigated at Solna were pronounced whipping boys or bullies. For several reasons, this figure is likely to be too low rather than an overestimate. First, many teachers—naturally enough—wanted to be generally cautious in making use of the pronounced category, and therefore some boys, who according to the peer ratings showed pronounced problems, were labeled by the teachers as less pronounced whipping boys or bullies. Second, the definition of a pronounced whipping boy was rather narrow insofar as it was confined to boys who had been the target of active aggression from others and over a fairly long period. The percentages would obviously have been higher if the definition of a whipping boy had included boys who were unpopular in the group, perhaps rejected and isolated but without being often attacked by the others. In sum, it can be concluded that an alarmingly high percentage of the boys studied were involved in whipping boy/bully problems.

The not uncommon notion that by and large it is the same boys who are both whipping boy and bully—although perhaps in somewhat different situations—found very little support in the present material. Only a very small percentage of the boys could really be considered as fluctuating between whipping boy and bully. Analyses of the boys' behavior characteristics (for their more psychological characteristics, see Chapter 7) also showed very marked differences between the different groups. All in all, this indicated that by and large quite different types of boys become whipping boys and bullies respectively. As a note of caution, it should perhaps be added that even if no support were obtained here for the idea that whipping boys and bullies are normally only "two sides of the same coin," the material analyzed so far has dealt primarily with the school setting and relations in this setting. It is, of course, conceivable that the whipping boys in more secure contexts attempted to retaliate for the suffering they had endured in the school setting.

SUMMARIZING DISCUSSION

After analyses of several different subject groups, it can be concluded that the teachers were able to make reliable assessments of the boys as whipping boys or bullies according to specified criteria. The peer ratings on different variables provided very strong evidence of the validity of the teachers' assessments.

To a great extent, these assessments measured what they were intended to measure. The follow-up investigation in grade 7, a year after the first part of the study was completed, showed that in large measure it was the same boys who were whipping boys/bullies in the seventh grade as in the sixth grade. From this finding, the conclusion can be drawn that it is not just anyone in a class who becomes a whipping boy or a bully. It is a matter of certain typical peer relations, and they often extend over long periods of time, that is, show a substantial degree of stability. These peer relations can be assessed by both teachers and peers with a considerable degree of certainty.

On the basis of the assessments made by the main teachers, the percentage of pronounced whipping boys in the grades could be estimated at approximately 5%, and the percentage of bullies was of about the same order. The percentage of boys with pronounced whipping boy/bully problems could thus be estimated as around 10%. For several reasons, this figure is likely to be an underestimate rather than an overestimate. If the boys assessed as less pronounced whipping boys or bullies are included, estimates in the vicinity of 20% are obtained. The above figures imply that, on the average, whipping boy/bully problems occured in every class. It should be added, however, that the variation from class to class was quite marked.

In order to give a more concrete idea of the significance of these results, one may argue as follows.

Solna is a town with approximately 55,000 inhabitants, and on January 1, 1975, it ranked 24th in size among the 278 Swedish municipalities. It has been demonstrated (e.g., by Klackenberg, 1971) that with regard to socioeconomic factors, Solna can be said to be representative not only of Greater Stockholm, but also, at least roughly, of any Swedish town. The organization of primary schooling in Solna shows no special features that can reasonably be assumed to affect the incidence of whipping boy/bully problems (see Chapter 5). About 20% of the entire country's approximately 975,000 primary-school pupils go to schools with less than 10 ordinary classes. In Solna, the corresponding figure was about 10% (of approximately 5,300 pupils). On the other hand, there are no very large schools in Solna. The largest school involved in the investigations had 32 classes and approximately 825 pupils. In the country as a whole, about 27% of the pupils go to schools with more than 29 ordinary classes, whereas the corresponding figure for Solna was approximately 16%. There is thus no overrepresentation of large school units in Solna. Several of the schools taking part in the investigation were small, having less than 200 pupils.

It is conceivable that the nearness of Solna to the center of Stockholm—and factors associated with this nearness—might contribute to relatively high frequency values for Solna. In the absence of reliable information on this point, however, the importance of these factors should perhaps not be overemphasized. It must be remembered that the percentage of primary-school pupils in small schools in the country—which might be thought to have lower frequencies—is fairly small. Furthermore, it should be recalled that approximately 60% of the population of Sweden live in towns with more than 30,000 inhabitants, and nearly 30% of the population live in towns with over 100,000 inhabitants.

Three grades—6, 7, and 8—are represented in the present studies, and no marked differences between these grades could be established. There are no special grounds for thinking that the other grades would have lower frequencies.

If the premises outlined above are accepted and, in addition, the estimated percentage of pronounced whipping boys is reduced from Solna's 5% to 3% for the whole country, one arrives at the result that approximately 15,000 boys in Sweden's primary schools are pronounced whipping boys in relation to their peers. In the same way, the number of bullies can be calculated to be roughly 15,000. The total number of boys with pronounced whipping boy/bully problems is thus about 30,000. If it is furthermore assumed that among girls the problems exist but are less frequent (and also may manifest themselves in somewhat different ways), one comes close to total estimates of 50,000 pupils. If boys and girls with less pronounced problems are included, the estimate comes to nearly 100,000 pupils, that is 1 pupil in 10. Children under school age and youths older than the primary school's top class (i.e., over approximately 16 years) are not included in these figures.

It must be emphasized that the frequencies given do not

pretend to be more than very rough estimates. And the main object of making the calculations has not been to provide more or less exact information about the incidence of these problems. Basically, the purpose has been to give concrete, if rough, figures on what can be established with considerable certainty: A very large number of children and youths in Sweden, at any rate in the ages from 7 to 16, are seriously involved in whipping boy/bully problems.

The previous analysis and conclusion receive considerable support from some recent Swedish publications in which the results from six independent studies on the frequency of whipping boy/bully problems ("mobbing") are reported. (Five of these studies are summarized in Pikas, 1975; see also Nihlén, 1976). In spite of somewhat varying definitions, different methods of data collection, and great variation in the population of the towns in which the schools were located—from 25,000 to 700,000 inhabitants—the results were fairly similar, centering on approximately 5% pronounced whipping boys, the same value as reported in the present chapter. The majority of these studies used classes from grades 6 to 9. In the most ambitious of these investigations (Nihlén, 1976), however, lower grades were also included, but no marked differences between the grades, from 3 to 9, could be established, the percentage values for boys varying between 3 and 7%. This study comprised approximately 2,000 pupils from a small town in the southern part of Sweden, having approximately 25,000 inhabitants, and the data were collected by means of a group-administered questionnaire (in which the pupils' anonymity was guaranteed). The definition of a whipping boy (target of "mobbing") presented to the pupils was based on the one given in this book (p. 34). All in all, although some caution must be exercised in interpreting the results from these studies, they are in general agreement with the findings reported in this chapter, and they lend additional credence to the analysis and the general conclusion presented in this section. Obviously, there are considerable whipping boy/bully problems in Swedish primary schools, and they seem to occur with at least roughly the same frequency under a variety of conditions.

The main points of this chapter can be summarized as follows.

- Teachers were able to make reliable assessments of school boys as whipping boys or bullies according to specified criteria. The peer ratings provided very strong support for the validity of the teachers's assessments.
- To a great extent, it was the same boys who were whipping boys/bullies in grade 6 and in grade 7, a year later, in spite of the fact that the large majority of the boys had new teachers and were in new schools. Clearly, the peer relations had a considerable degree of stability.
- The teacher and peer assessments gave very little support for the notion that it is usually the same boys who are both whipping boy and bully. On the whole, it seems to be quite different types of boys who become whipping boy and bully, respectively.
- In the Solna studies, grades 6–8, the percentage of pronounced whipping boys as well as of pronounced bullies could be estimated at 5%. The total percentage of boys with pronounced whipping boy/bully problems was thus approximately 10%. Based on certain assumptions, the number of boys with pronounced whipping boy/bully problems in Swedish primary schools can be estimated at approximately 30,000. Still higher figures are obtained if girls and pupils with less pronounced problems are included. It can be concluded that a very large number of children and youths in Swedish primary schools are seriously involved in whipping boy/bully problems.

5

WHIPPING BOY/BULLY PROBLEMS AND FACTORS IN THE SCHOOL SETTING

A further analysis of the data presented in the last chapter will now be of interest, first in order to examine whether whipping boy/bully problems are associated with factors in the school setting, that is, with factors in Sector A in the theory sketch. Is there any basis for the assumption, often made in Scandinavia, that mobbing problems increase in proportion to the size of the school? Are there more whipping boys in large classes? Does the teacher play any part in engendering whipping boy/bully problems in a class? Is there any relation between the group climate in a class and the incidence of whipping boys and bullies? These are some of the questions that will be studied in this chapter.

VARIABLES AND INSTRUMENTS

The data from the first Solna investigation, together with some of the follow-up data collected a year later in the seventh grade, have been the main source for the analyses reported in this chapter. The total percentage frequency of whipping boys and/or bullies was presented in Table 4 (p. 47). In this chapter, however, the analyses will concentrate on the incidence of whipping boys and/or bullies in the different classes; accordingly, the class, rather than particular boys, is the appropriate unit of analysis. The special classes are excluded from these analyses for several reasons: In general, they are very small (the average number of boys in each of the four special classes in the first Solna investigation was 5), they have specially trained teachers, and there is often variation in their composition. In all, 22 ordinary classes were included in the following analyses.

To increase the opportunities of discovering possibly meaningful relationships, the analyses were made with a considerable number of variables (dependent variables) taken separately and combined into composites. Six of the variables analyzed can be found in Table 5, with ranges and mean values. In addition to these six, the following variables were also studied: the same variables expressed as percentages of the number of boys and number of pupils in the class, respectively, and, further, variables

TABLE 5

Some Dependent Variables for
Incidence of Whipping Boy/Bully Problems in the Class[a]

Variable	Range	Mean
1. No. of pronounced whipping boys in class	0-2	.77
2. No. of pronounced bullies in class	0-3	.73
3. Sum (1 + 2)	0-5	1.50
4. No. of less pronounced + pronounced whipping boys in class	0-3	.95
5. No. of less pronounced + pronounced bullies in class	0-4	1.23
6. Sum (4 + 5)	0-6	2.18

[a]No. of classes = 22

4-6 in Table 5 weighted according to degree (pronounced = weight 2, less pronounced = weight 1). The sum variables, for instance, 3 and 6 in the table, were designed to provide a composite indicator of the degree of whipping boy/bully problems in a class.

Since the number of class units in the investigation was limited and some of the variables had somewhat skewed or irregular distributions, the material has been analyzed by more than one method: in part with ordinary product-moment correlations,[1] in part with phi correlations, that is, product-moment correlations for dichotomized variables (divided above/below the median), and for quite a number of variables, one-way analysis of variance was also used, generally with three categories in the independent variable (e.g., large, medium, and small schools). In this way, it was possible to discover and allow for "spurious relationships" that might appear in one of the methods of analysis as a consequence of, for example, special distribution characteristics. As a rule, only those results will be presented for which the different methods have shown similar trends. Thus what follows constitutes a selection of the more reliable findings from a substantial number of analyses.

In this connection, it should also be emphasized that even though the number of classes is not very great, the variable values for the individual classes have considerable reliability. For example, this is the case for the peer ratings and for the values for Our Class (attitude inventory, discussed below), where the variable value for a class is determined by several different assessors or by the majority of boys in the class.

Size of School

The first Solna investigation comprised all the 26 sixth-grade classes in Solna. These classes were distributed among 11 schools in 6 different areas (headmaster divisions). In the statistical analyses, the 22 ordinary classes from 10 different schools were included. The smallest school consisted of 6 classes and only

---

[1] Unless otherwise stated, the correlations reported in this and the following chapters are ordinary product-moment correlations.

132 pupils; the largest consisted of 32 classes and 824 pupils. The median was 14 classes and about 300 pupils.

In the follow-up investigation the next year, the boys had predominantly the same classmates. The 26 class groupings had thus been retained virtually unaltered, though there had been a limited amount of movement between the classes and also in and out. The boys in the two largest schools had continued in the same school buildings as in grade 6, while the rest had moved to new schools, usually larger or very much larger than those they had been in before. In the seventh grade, the number of schools had dropped to seven and the median number of classes per school was 20. The median number of pupils per schools had increased from around 300 to around 500.

Size of Class

All the 22 ordinary classes were mixed; that is, they included both boys and girls. The number of pupils varied from 19 to 30, with a mean value of 26. The number of boys in the classes varied from 6 to 15, but the large majority of the classes had 10 or more boys, with an average of 12. The product-moment correlation between the number of pupils and the number of boys in the class was .68.

Teacher Assessments

At the end of the interview with the main teacher, the following four questions were asked: (1) How is this class to work with as compared with other classes? (2) What are the peer relations in this class? (3) What is the attitude of the class to schoolwork? (4) How do you like being a teacher in today's schools?

The same questions were also answered by the woodwork teachers in the sixth grade, but only the answers to question 2 on the peer relations are included in the analyses. In the follow-up investigation of the seventh grade, only question 2 was put to the teachers.

Two psychologists, one of whom was the interviewer, scored the teachers' answers according to a 7-point scale (1 = very

positive or good; 7 = very negative or poor). The interjudge reliability of these independent assessments proved to be very good:
All correlations were higher than .90 (this analysis and the ones
that follow in this section are based on 22 classes).

The agreement between the assessments made by the main
teachers and by the woodwork teachers (the answers to question
2 as scored by the two psychologists) was only moderate,
$r = .41$), which implies that the two categories of teachers saw
partly different sides of the peer relations and/or viewed the
classes or the concept of peer relations somewhat differently.

The questions put to the teachers were designed to get an
impresssion of the following aspects: (1) the teacher's general
evaluation of the class, mainly from the work point of view, (2)
the peer relations, (3) the general attitude of the class to
schoolwork, and (4) the teachers' general satisfaction with the
teaching profession. As might be expected, positive and in most
cases high correlations among the four variables appeared. In
particular, the first three variables, concerning somewhat different sides of the main teacher's general view of the class, were
highly intercorrelated, with an average of .81. The correlation
among these variables and the teacher's general satisfaction with
the profession (question 4) was also positive, though lower, with
an average of .47.[2]

As stated, the new main teachers were asked to assess the
peer relations of the class in the seventh grade. The correlation
between the assessments made by the main teachers in the sixth
grade and in the seventh grade was .59; the average of the main
teachers' and the woodwork teachers' assessments in the sixth
grade correlated .68 with the main teachers' assessments in the
seventh grade. These are surprisingly high values when all
correlation-lowering factors are taken into account: In addition
to the fact that a year had passed, and a certain, though limited,
change in pupils had occurred in some classes, it should be
pointed out that the teachers in grade 6 and 7 were different
(with one exception), that the new teachers had taught the boys
for relatively few periods per week, and that, in general, the

---

[2] The relationships reported are also dependent on common method
variance.

teacher assessments in each grade were less than perfectly reliable (each teacher assessed only one class). The results show that there was considerable stability over time in the quality of the peer relations as evaluated by the teachers and that different teachers (at any rate, the main teachers) apprehended the characteristics of the peer relations in a class in much the same way. The high correlation between the attitude of the class to schoolwork and the peer relations (see above) suggests, however, that the teachers' assessments of the peer relations were perhaps associated more with the general attitude of the class to school-work and to their teachers than directly with the peer relations. The fact that the teacher variable for the peer relations did not correlate significantly with any of the peer-rated variables Start Fights, Tease, and Aggression Target supports this interpretation (for significance at the .05 level, a phi or $r = .42$ is needed).

Our Class

The attitude inventory, Our Class, constructed by Johannesson (1966), originally contained 93 items. For the present investigation, the following changes were made, with Johannesson's permission: The number of items was limited to 30 (of which 4 were fillers), some questions about negative attitude toward the teacher were reconstructed, and the format of the inventory was altered somewhat.

The items were selected on the basis of Johannesson's factor analyses, which had given four (or three) factors (Johannesson, 1966). Factor analyses ($n = 247$) of the abbreviated inventory used in this investigation produced much the same results as Johannesson's. I have chosen to employ four main dimensions here, but dimensions III and IV (see below) were so highly intercorrelated that it would have been possible to combine them into one dimension (after "reversing" one or the other). The four dimensions or scales can be designated as follows:

   I. *Negative attitude to schoolwork* (6 items, e.g., I get bored in school; I think we have to learn so much in school that isn't useful).

II. *Poor peer relations* (6 items, e.g., in our class the pupils tease each other; I feel lonely and isolated at school).

III. *Positive attitude to teachers* (7 items, e.g., our teachers are kind; our teachers help us a lot with our work).

IV. *Negative attitude to teachers* (7 items, e.g., it is difficult to discuss anything with our teachers; the teachers are not very fair).

The items in scales III and IV referred throughout to several teachers ("our teachers," etc.) but bearing in mind that most of the teaching in the sixth grade was done by the main teachers, it can be assumed that the boys' answers reflected to a great degree their view of these teachers.

For each item, there were five response alternatives (from "hardly ever" to "as a rule"), scored 1–5. Simple sum (or mean) variables were formed by adding the scores of the items constituting a scale. An average value for each class and variable was formed by using the scores of the boys present when the inventory was administered to the class in question.

A total of 247 boys out of the 274 boys in the ordinary classes filled out the Our Class inventory. Of the 27 absent boys, 7 belonged to the special group of bullies (p. 43). Two of the 7 were in the special classes, which are not included in the following analyses, and the remaining 5 were distributed over the classes in such a way that the effects on the mean values of the classes concerned may be considered negligible.

The internal consistency reliability (alpha coefficients) of the four scales varied between .67 and .82, with an average of .75. It should be noted, however, that the class mean values on each dimension were based on quite a number of individuals, 11 on the average. This fact, of course, increases considerably the reliability of the mean values, which are the units to be used in the analyses in this chapter.

The intercorrelations between the scales appear in Table 6. Classes with a negative attitude to their teachers also had a negative attitude to schoolwork. In the same way, though less markedly, classes with poor relations according to Our Class

TABLE 6

Intercorrelations (Product-Moment)
between the Scales in the Attitude Inventory Our Class

Scale	II	III	IV
I. Negative attitude to schoolwork	.34	−.44	.66
II. Poor peer relations		−.31	.40
III. Positive attitude to teachers			−.88
IV. Negative attitude to teachers			

Note. The correlations are based on 22 class mean values, and each class mean is based on the values of approximately 11 boys.

tended to have a more negative attitude to their teachers as well as to schoolwork.

As regards the *validity* of the scales, the following can be adduced. Scales I, III, and IV concerning negative attitude to schoolwork and teachers (scale III "reversed" in the following) showed such similar patterns of correlation with the relevant variables that in this context they can be regarded as approximately equivalent. These scales had clear positive relationships with the three teacher variables, teachers's general evaluation of the class, general attitude of the class to schoolwork, and peer relations (p. 59). The average correlations (for I, III, and IV) were .48, .40, and .46, respectively. Thus, in classes where the boys had a more negative attitude to schoolwork and teachers, the main teachers also thought that the class attitude to schoolwork was more negative; moreover, the teachers' general evaluation of the class tended to be more negative in such classes. A more negative attitude to schoolwork/teachers according to the boys was also associated with poor peer relations according to the teachers.

Negative attitude to schoolwork/teachers correlated, however, only weakly or not at all with the peer-rated variables Start Fights, Tease, and Aggression Target. The peer-rated variable Verbal Protest (against teachers), on the other hand, showed stronger relationships with the Our Class variables: The average correlation for I, III, and IV was .38, with .47 as the highest correlation value, reasonably enough with the variable, Negative attitude to teachers (IV).

Poor peer relations, as indicated by the Our Class variable,

PROBLEMS AND FACTORS IN THE SCHOOL SETTING

correlated close to zero with the main teachers' assessment of the peer relations and also with the other teacher variables. The Our Class variable covaried, however, fairly strongly with the peer variables Start Fights, Tease, and Aggression Target, the average correlation being .52. This association is easy to understand: More negative peer relations, as measured by Our Class, should correlate positively with the average (class) level of peer-rated variables reflecting how much the boys in the class fight and/or tease each other or are the target of aggresssion by their classmates. It should be noted that the two sets of data were obtained by means of basically different methods.

The above correlation patterns support the following generalizations. Negative attitude to schoolwork/teachers, according to the boys' own reports, covaried meaningfully with similar variables as assessed by the teachers. The fairly close relationship between poor peer relations as measured by Our Class and three of the peer-rated variables must be interpreted as evidence that these variables reflected at least some of the same aspects of the peer relations in a class. On the whole, the results testify that the instruments and variables discussed so far (with the exception of the teacher assessments of the peer relations) measured essentially what they were intended to measure.

Peer Ratings

The general procedure for collecting the peer ratings has been discussed earlier (p. 24). Here I shall add only that the reliability of the average values for the *individuals* in a class has often been found to lie in the region of .70-.95 (see Olweus, 1969, 1975, 1977a) when using three or four assessors of the same variables as those in the present investigation. It can therefore be accepted with certitude that the mean values *for the boys in a whole class,* judged by the average four raters, were very reliable.

The correlation between Start Fights and Tease was .53 across the 22 classes. These two variables had positive but lower relationships with Aggression Target and Verbal Protest: The average correlations here were .17 and .36, respectively.

For 8 of the classes taking part and for two of the variables—Start Fights and Aggression Target—peer ratings collected a year later, in grade 7, were also available. In spite of the fact that these later ratings were made by only *one* boy (who did not take part in the sixth grade ratings) in each class and thus had limited reliability, the correlation with the average ratings from grade 6 was high: The mean correlation across the 8 classes (a total *n* of 76) was .76 for Start Fights and .53 for Aggression Target. Thus the peer relations as reflected in these variables were noticeably stable over a period of 1 year. The results are in general agreement with those presented earlier for a time interval of 6 months (Olweus, 1973a) and with the findings from the more comprehensive follow-up study covering the 3-year interval from grade 6 to grade 9, to be reported on in more detail in Chapter 7 (pp. 125–130). The follow-up study included 18 classes (*n* = 201) and four peer-rated variables.

Indicators of the Group Climate

Some of the instruments and variables described above were chosen with the object of obtaining measures or indicators of the "group climate." As several authors have pointed out (e.g., Sjölund, 1972) concepts such as group climate and social atmosphere have been used vaguely and in different senses by different authors. This has led to different indicators of the concept in question. In the present study, the need was to find indicators of the more habitual group climate characteristic of a somewhat longer period of time, to be related to the incidence of whipping boy/bully problems. Another point of departure was that the boys themselves could be assumed to have the best information on these relations with the teachers as well as with classmates.

The analyses already reported as well as theoretical considerations made it natural to study the group climate in two different main areas. The first concerns the degree of tension and conflict between the boys in the class and the teachers and what they represent. Natural indicators would seem to be scales I, III, and IV in Our Class (Negative attitude to schoolwork, Positive attitude to teachers and Negative attitude to teachers) and possibly also the peer-rated variable Verbal Protest (against teacher). In addition, the teacher assessments of the class might be used as indicators but with greater uncertainty for this particular purpose.

For the second main area, which concerns the degree of tension and conflict between the boys in the class (negative peer relations), suitable indicators would seem to be scale II in Our Class, Poor peer relations, and the peer variables Start Fights, Tease, and Aggression Target. The three peer variables in particular may correspond to Lewin's perception (1936) of the term social atmosphere. The degrees of friendliness, hostility, and tension are central characteristics of Lewin's concept.

As appeared from the previous analyses, there existed some positive but rather weak relationships between the indicators of the group climate in the two main areas. The predominating impression was that they were largely independent of each other.

SIZE OF CLASS AND SCHOOL

Results

No systematic relationships could be discovered between the number of whipping boys and/or bullies per class and the size of the class, either in terms of the number of pupils or the number of boys in the class. For instance, when the classes were divided into three groups—small (less than 12 boys, $n = 8$ classes), medium (12-14 boys, $n = 9$ classes), and large (15 boys, $n = 5$ classes)—for the sum variable (number of pronounced + less pronounced whipping boys and bullies), $F(2, 19) = 1.33$, $p > .05$. The corresponding F value for this variable expressed as a percentage of the number of boys in the class was 1.87, $p > .05$. There appeared to be a slight tendency for small *and* large classes to have somewhat more problems, but as is evident from the statistical analyses, this tendency was not strong enough to reach significance. It should be noted, however, that although the number of boys in the classes ranged from 6 to 15, the majority had between 10 and 15 boys. Thus the variation in the class sizes studied was not particularly great.

The size of the school also did not show any systematic

relationships with the whipping boy/bully variables. For example, when the classes coming from small (132-281 pupils, $n = 6$ classes from 5 schools), medium (295-336 pupils, $n = 9$ classes from 3 schools), and large schools (599-824 pupils, $n = 7$ classes from 2 schools) were compared in one-way analyses of variance with respect to the variables listed in Table 7, F (2, 19) = 1.54, .18, and .13, respectively, $p > .05$.[3] And for the sum variable (number of pronounced + less pronounced whipping boys and bullies) expressed as a percentage of the number of the boys in the class, $F = .76, p > .05$.

Furthermore, examination of classes coming from the same school unit revealed a very marked variation in amount of whipping boy/bully problems. Whereas, for instance, a particular class had no problems at all, a parallel class from the same school showed very pronounced problems that had lasted for several years. In addition, no systematic trends appeared when the individual schools were compared according to size.[4]

Essentially the same results as reported above for grade 6 were obtained when the size of the school and class units in grade 7 was related to the degree of whipping boy/bully problems in the respective classes.

The fact that 10 classes were transferred to larger school units in the transition from grade 6 to grade 7 provided an

---

[3] In these analyses, the classes were regarded as independent units. If there were dependencies between the classes within a school—which hardly seems likely in view of the marked variation in whipping boy/bully problems between classes coming from the same school (see above text)—this is most likely to have increased the probability of obtaining significant differences between schools of different sizes. It should also be noted that very small differences in the mean values were obtained for the three groups of schools, if the school rather than the class was used as the unit of analysis (in which case an average value was formed for each school having more than one class).

[4] In addition, a comparison of whipping boys coming from relatively small (less than 300 pupils) and relatively large (more than 300 pupils) schools showed small and unsystematic differences in variables concerning various psychological and behavioral characteristics (Sector C, Chapter 7)—according to the boys themselves, their mothers, and their peers. Similar results were obtained for bullies coming from small and large schools, respectively.

TABLE 7

Relationship between Size of the School
and Mean Number of Whipping Boys (Wh)/Bullies (B) per Class

	Average number of pronounced + less pronounced Wh/class	Average number of pronounced + less pronounced B/class	Average number of pronounced + less pronounced Wh+B/class
Classes from small schools (132–285 pupils) $n^a = 6$	1.00	1.33	2.33
Classes from medium schools (295–336 pupils) $n = 9$	.67	1.33	2.00
Classes from large schools (599–824 pupils) $n = 7$	1.29	1.00	2.29
F $(df = 2, 19)$	1.54 n.s.	.18 n.s.	.13 n.s.

[a] The n values indicate number of classes.

additional opportunity to study whether there was any relationship between the degree of whipping boy/bully problems and
the size of the school. Five classes were transferred to schools
more than twice as large (from under 300 pupils to over 600
pupils) and the other 5 to schools about 50% larger (from 275
pupils to over 425 pupils). No systematic trend toward an
increase in the number of whipping boys and/or bullies could be
found in these classes as compared with the same classes a year
earlier. Rather, there was a slight (nonsignificant) reduction, and
the problems in the other 12 classes, which continued in the
same school buildings or moved into schools of the same size,
remained at approximately the same level.

Comments

The results indicate that neither the size of the class nor the number of boys in the class was of importance for the degree of whipping boy/bully problems in the class, that is, within the ranges studied and for the grades concerned. Although the variation in class size was not particularly great, it is definitely unusual to find much greater variation in this respect in Swedish schools. It may thus be concluded that mobbing problems occurred in small as well as in large classes and to about the same extent.

The common hypothesis that the incidence of mobbing problems increases in proportion to the size of the school is probably based on the following assumptions. The accumulation of many individuals in one place engenders more tensions and conflicts. Furthermore, the setting in large schools leads to more impersonal relations and perhaps to greater indifference to the value of other individuals, which should contribute to an increase in the frequency of whipping boy/bully problems. Although these assumptions may seem reasonable, a number of empirical analyses failed to support the hypothesis in question.[5] And it should be noted that the variation in school size was quite marked—from 132 to 824 pupils. The largest school had more than six times as many pupils as the smallest.

The results also showed that there was little empirical reason for regarding a school as a homogeneous unit from the point of view relevant here: The variation between classes from the same school was generally quite pronounced in the variables studied.

The results presented concerned grades 6 and 7 in schools with a certain range of variation as regards number of pupils, the

---

[5] Due to the great practical and methodological difficulties involved, the general aggression level was not studied in terms of the frequency of aggressive events occurring during a number of time periods. Such a measure, however, would probably be substantially correlated with the typical aggression level as measured by the average peer-rating values per class, in particular on the variables Start Fights and Tease. It is therefore of interest to know that, as with the whipping boy/bully variables, no systematic differences were found between schools of different sizes on these two or the other peer-rated variables.

largest school having slightly more than 800 pupils. The assumed relationship with school size might have been found (at least in part) if very large schools (e.g., 1,000 or more pupils) had been included in the investigation. In this connection, however, the following facts should be emphasized: (1) Only 20% of primary school pupils in Sweden (grades 1–9) go to schools larger than the schools included in this investigation. (2) The results show that even very small schools may have marked whipping boy/bully problems.

The findings from the present study are in agreement with the results obtained in a comprehensive Norwegian investigation, studying somewhat related variables in seventh-grade classes from 29 different schools (Øygarden, Lunde, & Jørgensen, 1971). In this investigation, no systematic relationships were found between size of the school (and the class) and several "discipline" variables assessed by the teachers, including frequency of problems concerning peer relations (e.g., bullying other children). The largest school had only about 450 pupils, but the range was great, and very small schools with around 50 pupils were also included.

Although systematic relationships between school size and certain variables have been demonstrated in some studies (e.g., Baird, 1969; Barker & Gump, 1964), it should be noted that the variables studies (such as participation in extracurricular activities, achievement, etc.) have been very different from those of interest here. In addition, it is obvious that even when a systematic relationship with school size is found, such a finding is open to a number of different interpretations that must be checked before any causal conclusions can be drawn.

On the basis of the empirical results obtained and the considerations discussed, the most reasonable conclusion is that the size of the school, in itself, was not an important factor for the appearance and the degree of whipping boy/bully problems.[6]

[6] A possible explanation of the common opinion that there is relatively more mobbing in large schools is: If the average number of whipping boys and/or bullies per class is about the same in large and small schools (as the above results suggest), the absolute number of whipping boys and/or bullies will be greater in large schools since these contain more classes; this may give the impression of relatively more mobbing in larger schools, a kind of "optical illusion."

This conclusion, however, must not be interpreted as an argument for building large school units. Here, the size of the school has been studied only in relation to mobbing problems, and from other points of view many grounds may be found for having small or medium-sized schools. The results, however, indicate that one must look for factors other than the size of the school when attempting to explain why whipping boy/bully problems arise.

THE GROUP CLIMATE

The next stage in the analyses concerns the group climate. The relations to teachers/schoolwork (first main area) will be treated first, followed by the peer relations (second main area). The conclusions drawn, however, will be based on the combined results from both these areas.

Results

Relations to Teachers/Schoolwork

It might be hypothesized that the teacher's general way of conducting the work of the class and his or her own satisfaction with the profession would be of importance for the appearance of whipping boy/bully problems in a class. Strict, negative, unfair, or dissatisfied teachers might engender a high level of tension and conflict in a class, which in turn could lead to or intensify whipping boy/bully problems among the peers. The investigations of Lewin, Lippitt, and White (1939) may be referred to in this connection.

The natural starting point for testing such a hypothesis is scale IV, Negative attitude to teacher(s), in Our Class. High values on this scale mean that the boys regard the teachers as strict, demanding, unfair, difficult to talk to, and so on ("authoritarian"). No systematic positive relationships between this variable and the variables for whipping boy/bully problems were found. For example, the correlation with variable 3 in Table 5 (p. 56), the sum of pronounced whipping boys and pronounced bullies in the class, was .18 (phi), whereas the corresponding value for variable 6 in the same table, which also includes the less pronounced whipping boys and bullies, was .06. It might be possible to trace a weak tendency to a negative relationship between the whipping boy variables and the Our Class variable, and this is directly incompatible with the hypothesis mentioned phi $= -.38$ with the variable number of pronounced whipping boys in a class; phi $= -.20$ with number of pronounced whipping boys + less pronounced whipping boys. Roughly the same results were obtained for the peer-rated variable Verbal Protest as for the Our Class variable.

Scale I in Our Class, Negative attitude to schoolwork, did not show any systematic relationships, either, with the whipping boy/bully variables. The correlations throughout were close to zero.

As mentioned, it might also be hypothesized that teachers who were dissatisfied with and negative toward their profession might give rise to irritation and negative reactions in the class[7] that indirectly could increase the probability of whipping boy/bully problems arising. A clear relationship was also found between the teachers' dissatisfaction with their profession and a negative attitude to the teachers according to Our Class, phi $= .55$, and this is not inconsistent with the first part of the reasoning above. However, the degree of the teachers' dissatisfaction with their profession as well as the attitude to the teachers as measured by Our Class correlated around zero with the whipping boy/bully variables, which is thus incompatible with the hypothesis in question.

The teacher's general evaluation of the class from the work point of view and the assessment of the attitude of the class to schoolwork—two variables that were highly intercorrelated—showed positive relationships with the whipping boy/bully variables, most markedly with the latter. For instance, the phi correlations between the teacher variables mentioned and the sum variable number of pronounced bullies + less pronounced bullies were .38 and .52. With the bully variable expressed as a

---

[7] The reasoning can also be reversed: If the attitude of the class is negative, this will affect the teacher and make him or her less satisfied with the profession.

percentage of the number of boys in the class, the values were .37 and .54. Corresponding correlations for the whipping boy variables were also positive but noticeably lower. In view of the other results reported in this section (between negative attitude to teachers and schoolwork in Our Class, the peer-rated variable Verbal Protest, and the teachers' satisfaction with their profession, on one hand, and the whipping boy/bully variables on the other), the following interpretation of the correlations seems by far the most reasonable: In the teachers' opinions, classes with, in particular, a relatively large number of bullies had a more negative attitude to schoolwork and were more difficult to work with.

Relations with Peers

One of the indicators of negative peer relations, Poor peer relations as indicated by Scale II in Our Class, showed no systematic relationships with the whipping boy/bully variables. The two peer-rated variables Start Fights and Tease, however, which correlated fairly highly with the scale Poor peer relations, were clearly related to the incidence of whipping boys/bullies in the class. Sum variable 6 in Table 5, number of pronounced + less pronounced whipping boys and bullies, correlated .37 with Start Fights and .55 with Tease. When this sum variable was related to the number of boys in the class (as a percentage), these correlations amounted to .45 and .64. These two sum variables correlated .55 and .64, respectively, with the sum of the two peer-rated variables Start Fights and Tease (all correlations in this paragraph are phi coefficients).

Group Climate—Summarizing Discussion

In evaluating and interpreting the results obtained, it is important to take the whole pattern of relationships and lack of relationships into consideration. In view of the complexity of the problems under study, isolated findings obviously have only little value as evidence. It is also clear that some of the results presented earlier have a direct significance for the problems under discussion. There are thus grounds for examining some of these findings again, but from a somewhat different angle.

As regards the first main area, relations to teachers/schoolwork, the following points should be emphasized.

1. There were no systematic, positive relationships between degree of negative attitude to teacher(s) or schoolwork (according to Our Class) and the incidence of whipping boy/bully problems in the class.

2. The teacher's degree of satisfaction with his or her profession did not covary systematically with the incidence of whipping boy/bully problems in the class.

3. A negative attitude to teacher(s) or schoolwork (according to Our Class) was not systematically related to the peer-rated variables Start Fights and Tease. These variables, however, were found to be associated with the incidence of whipping boy/bully problems (see point 6).

4. The teacher designations of whipping boys and bullies in the sixth grade showed a high degree of agreement with corresponding designations in the seventh grade: For instance, 81% of the pronounced bullies and 69% of the pronounced whipping boys in grade 6 were selected as bullies and whipping boys, respectively, one year later. It should be emphasized that these results were obtained in spite of the fact that nearly all the classes had new teachers in grade 7.

5. The teachers' assessments of the peer relations in the sixth grade—which in reality seemed to be an assessment of the general attitude of the class to schoolwork and the teachers—covaried markedly with the corresponding assessments in the seventh grade. It is essential for both this point and the previous one that the new main teachers presumably differed from those in the sixth grade in a number of ways, for example, in methods of teaching, satisfaction with their profession, and personal circumstances, and obviously also as people.

As regards the second main area, peer relations, the following points may be added.

6. Systematic, positive relationships were found between two of the peer-rated variables, Start Fights and Tease—which were used as indicators of the degree of conflict and tension between boys in the class—and the incidence of whipping boy/bully problems.

7. The follow-up data for two of the peer-rated variables, Start Fights and Aggression Target, showed that the peer relations measured in this manner were remarkably stable from grade 6 to grade 7—despite the fact that in grade 7, nearly all the classes had new teachers and many were in new schools. The high degree of stability of the peer relations, in spite of certain environmental changes, will also be substantiated in the more comprehensive follow-up study covering a 3-year interval, to be reported on in Chapter 7. The results from this study will lend additional support to the conclusions to be drawn in the following sections.

Three conclusions can be drawn from this pattern of results. First, however, it must be emphasized that these conclusions are likely to be valid only under "typical, existing conditions," that is, with the variation in, for example, the teacher's teaching methods, attitude, and behavior toward the pupils that normally can be expected to occur in the year groups in question. Thus the conclusions do not imply that things have to be that way. I shall return to this point in Chapter 9.

The following conclusions can then be formulated.

1. The whipping boy/bully problems were largely bound up with the character of the interpersonal relations among the boys in the class.
2. These interpersonal relations were quite stable over time.
3. The relations to the teachers and to schoolwork seemed to be of minor significance for these interpersonal relations as well as for the appearance and the degree of whipping boy/bully problems in a class.

Let us begin by examining conclusion 3, which is formulated as a statement on a lack of relationship and is based partly on the absence of relationships (zero-relationships) stated in several of the points listed. Of course, it can always be maintained— often with good reason—that the absence of relationships is only a consequence of inadequate or insensitive instruments and methods. The conclusion drawn, however, is based not only on these points but also and to a great degree on another type of result: There was a substantial agreement from grade 6 to grade 7 both as regards peer ratings (also from grade 6 to grade 9), designation of whipping boys and bullies, and in the teacher assessments of peer relations—in spite of the fact that nearly all the teachers in the seventh grade were new. If the teachers and their conduct of schoolwork had been of real importance for the character of the boys' interpersonal relations, in the sense relevant here, or for the whipping boy/bully problems in a class, there would have been reason to expect far less stability on the points mentioned. These results in combination with the zero-relationships mentioned, obtained with reasonably valid methods, provide strong support for the conclusion given.

This conclusion may appear to conflict with results from some group psychological research, especially the frequently cited investigations by Lewin et al. (1939). In these studies, the form of leadership exercised by the group's formal leader was found to affect the psychological climate and the peer relations in the group. However, for methodological[8] and other reasons— the groups were much smaller and of a different character and permanence than an ordinary school class—it seems very doubtful whether the results obtained by the Lewin group can be applied to the situation in an ordinary school class (see also Ausubel, 1968; Wallen & Travers, 1963). More generally, it may also be pointed out that research on the possible effects of teachers on peer relations has not been particularly lively and has produced ambiguous results (e.g., Sechrest, 1964; Watson, 1965, p. 586). Thus, on further consideration of the results, it is hardly surprising that the peer relations relevant here were found to be fairly independent of such factors as the attitude of the class to the teachers and to schoolwork. The results suggest that the peer group functioned to a considerable extent as a "closed system" with its own forms of interaction, which agrees with general experience about the growing importance of the peer group with increasing age. It should, however, be pointed out that more transient effects of the behavior and reactions of the teachers have not been the object of study in the present work.

[8] The methodological weaknesses of these studies are so great that it is doubtful whether the studies can constitute a basis for any conclusions at all (see footnote, p. 183, and Sechrest, 1964).

It is, for instance, possible that a temporary conflict with a teacher can for a time exacerbate an existing mobbing problem in a class.

It may also be added that the third conclusion, about the limited influence of the teachers on the peer relations under discussion, can be assumed to be valid primarily for school classes with somewhat older boys. It is likely that the importance of the teacher in this area *may* be considerably greater in children's earlier years at school.

Conclusion 2, on the permanence of the interpersonal relations, was already formulated in the last chapter. It has, however, been confirmed and strengthened by the data on the stability of the peer ratings.

Conclusion 1—that the whipping boy/bully problems were largely bound up with the character of the interpersonal relations among the boys in the class—may at first seem evident but should not be understood in this manner after the comments on conclusion 3. By definition, whipping boy/bully problems concern certain peer relations. However, as already discussed, it is possible that factors basic to the appearance of the problems could lie outside the peer group, for instance, in the way the teacher conducts the class. As appears from the analyses, hypotheses of this type were not supported by the results obtained.

In one sense, conclusion 1 is quite general, and the results in point 6 in the summary on group climate imply in the first place that classes with much fighting and teasing between the boys also had more marked whipping boy/bully problems. This finding is easy to understand, though hardly evident, but the results do not say much about the mechanisms of the problem. To gain a deeper understanding on this point, the boys assessed by the teachers as whipping boys and/or bullies must now be studied more closely. If such boys show special characteristics, valuable information about the mechanisms in question might ensue. Analyses of a number of such conceivable characteristics— individual factors, primarily in Sectors B and C in the theory sketch—will be presented in the following two chapters.

Yet another point about the first conclusion should be made. The word "largely" is also included in order to convey that not all whipping boy/bully problems are confined to the relations between the boys in the class. It appeared from the descriptions given by the teachers that boys from other classes or girls in the same class could also be involved, but this was exceptional.

Finally, to avoid misunderstanding, I wish to emphasize that the results do *not* imply that teachers are not in a position to make an important contribution to the elimination or reduction of the incidence of mobbing in the schools. In the final chapter, I shall return to this point and to the whole question of remedial measures.

The main results of this chapter can be summarized as follows.

- The size of the school, in itself, was not an important factor for the appearance and the degree of whipping boy/bully problems.
- Neither was the size of the class or the number of boys in the class of importance in these respects.
- The whipping boy/bully problems were largely bound up with the character of the interpersonal relations among the boys in the class.
- These interpersonal relations were quite stable over time.
- The relations to the teachers and to schoolwork seemed to be of minor significance, both for these interpersonal relations and for the appearance and the degree of whipping boy/bully problems in a class.

6

EXTERNAL DEVIATIONS

As already mentioned, in the Swedish public debate on possible mechanisms of mobbing, external deviations in the whipping boy, the victim of mobbing, have been considered a decisive factor: The victims are fat children, immigrant children, children whose appearance is different or who are oddly dressed. And it has been assumed that such deviations to a great extent directly cause the mobbing: The difference in itself, the deviance from the pattern of the group, creates tension and irritation in the group, with mobbing as a consequence. In this chapter, I shall look more closely at this aspect of the problem—Sector B in the theory sketch.

THE TEACHER ASSESSMENTS OF DEVIANCE

Method

The following analyses are based on the data from the first and second Solna investigations of grade 6.

After the main teachers had picked out possible whipping boys, bullies, and well-adjusted boys in the class, they were asked to consider whether the boy concerned was "unusual or deviant as compared with boys in general with respect to appearance, dress, or manner. For instance, is he unusually small or fat for his age? Is his way of speaking peculiar? Is he oddly dressed? Also include positive deviations, for example, that he looks very nice, is unusually strong, or particularly gifted." As a guide, the teacher was given a checklist of 14 characteristics. On this, the teacher was to mark whether the boy deviated much, somewhat, or not at all from other boys. (Because of the relatively low frequencies, the first two options were combined into one category: deviant.)

The checklist was designed to cover external deviations only, that is, deviations of such a nature that they were relatively apparent to people in the boy's vicinity and especially to his peers. The checklist cited the following 14 characteristics: physical handicap, sight (e.g., eyeglasses), hearing, speech (language), obesity, size (primarily small), physical strength I (weak), physical strength II (strong), appearance, color of skin, personal hygiene, facial expression (e.g., grimacing), posture, and dress. In addition, the teacher was asked to rate the boy's ability to profit from instruction as poor, average, or good. This last rating, which did not refer to external deviance, will be dealt with in Chapter 7. If a "non-Swedish" boy spoke broken Swedish or had a different-colored skin, this was recorded in the categories given above, but in order to get a clearer picture of the situation for the "foreign" boys, a special analysis was undertaken, which will be reported on separately.

As the instructions made clear, teachers were to record both positive and negative deviations. There were two grounds for this. One was to make sure that the attention of the teachers was not fixed on negative aspects only. The other was that positive deviations were of interest in themselves. Negative deviation meant chiefly deviations that boys of the same age might regard as negative or irritating, a minus.

In the first Solna investigation, teacher assessments of this type were made for the boys selected by the main teachers as whipping boys, bullies, or well-adjusted boys. In the second Solna investigation, assessments were collected not only for the specially selected boys but also for all the boys in six classes, 80 boys in all (representing the six headmaster divisions), the object being to provide a comparison or control group for the special groups in both the first and the second Solna investigations.

The following analyses were carried out:

1. Comparison of deviations and absence of deviations, respectively, for 19 whipping boys (information was lacking on 2), 21 bullies from the first Solna investigation (see p. 43) and a control group of 40 boys chosen at random from the 80 boys in the second Solna investigation.
2. The same comparisons as above, but for 22 whipping boys and 18 bullies from the second Solna investigation, and 45 boys selected at random from the 80 after whipping boys and bullies had been removed from this group. These 45 boys formed a somewhat "purer" control group than the first insofar as the group did not contain any whipping boys or bullies (the first randomly selected group contained 3 whipping boys and 4 bullies).

    The well-adjusted group in the first Solna investigation—22 boys (see p. 46)—were also included in several analyses, but the results for this group will be referred to only briefly.

Statistical analyses were carried out separately for each of the 14 characteristics and also for some composite variables that appeared to be of special interest. These were: physical defect (comprising the first 4 characteristics), appearance + dress + personal hygiene, "body build" (fat and/or small), and some others. The analyses were carried out for three groups together and also in the form of paired comparisons: whipping boys against control boys, bullies against control boys, and in some cases whipping boys against bullies. With respect to the problems posed initially in this chapter, the comparisons between the whipping boys and the control group are obviously of greatest interest.

The results for the two sets of groups described above were largely in agreement. Accordingly, certain tables will be presented that are based on the joint total of 41 whipping boys and 39 bullies. In these analyses, the control group of 45 boys—the one that had no whipping boys or bullies—will be employed.

The statistical analyses were carried out with the χ^2 test. In fourfold tables (2 × 2) with expected frequencies below five, Yates' correction for continuity was applied. As a measure of the strength of the association, the contingency coefficient C was used, the maximum value of which is .71 in 2 × 2 tables and .82 in 3 × 3 tables (e.g., McNemar, 1968). As a check, the probability of the differences in the 2 × 2 tables being random was also calculated by means of Fisher's exact probabilities test. The results of these calculations agreed with the χ^2 analyses.

Results

Table 8 shows some typical results from the first Solna investigation. Some of the boys showed negative deviations, but the large majority were not deviant—and this was true of all three groups. A tendency to more deviations can be traced in the whipping boys, but it was weak and nonsignificant, particularly with regard to obesity.

TABLE 8

Incidence of Deviation
for Obesity and Speech for Whipping Boys (Wh),
Control Boys (C), and Bullies (B).
Data from the First Solna Investigation, Grade 6

	Obesity				Speech		
	Nondeviant	Deviant (fat)	No. of boys		Nondeviant	Deviant	No. of boys
Wh	15	4	19	Wh	12	7	19
C	33	7	40	C	34	6	40
B	18	3	21	B	15	6	21
Total			80				80

$\chi^2 = .32$ $\chi^2 = 3.76$
p = not significant p = not significant

None of the paired comparisons Wh-C, B-C were significant, but there was a tendency toward a significant difference for Wh-C with regard to Speech, $p = .12$

Similar results were obtained for most of the characteristics listed even if one or two significant differences were found in either of the investigations. Thus the whipping boys were more deviant with regard to posture than the control group in the second Solna investigation, $p < .01$, $C = .31$, but this difference did not appear in the first Solna investigation. In the same way, whipping boys were assessed in the second investigation as more negatively deviant with respect to appearance, $p < .005$, $C = .36$, but this was far less marked (not significant) in the first investigation. These results might suggest that whipping boys generally were more deviant, but in somewhat different characteristics in the two investigations. Accordingly, it was desirable to form a more comprehensive, composite variable indicating nondeviance on the one hand, and deviation in *1 or more of the 14 characteristics*, on the other. The whipping boy group, however, did not contain significantly more deviant boys than the control group for this composite variable either. This applied to both investigations.

A more refined measure of the *degree of deviance* might be obtained by classifying the boys into three categories—nondeviant, deviant in 1 or 2 characteristics, and deviant in 3 or more characteristics. The results are given in Table 9.

The analyses were carried out on the total number of whipping boys and bullies in the two investigations. It appears from the table that there were more boys with deviations in the whipping boy group than in the control group even if the difference was not great. The bullies had fewer deviations than either the whipping boys ($p < .01$) or the control group (tendency). It is also worth noting how large a number of the boys were assessed as negatively deviant in one way or another: 90% of the whipping boys, 73% of the control group, and 54% of the bullies. By way of comparison, the corresponding percentage for the well-adjusted boys was 29%.

Physical strength, the only characteristic for which the two investigations yielded clear and concordant results has yet to be considered. The whipping boys were generally assessed as negatively deviant with respect to physical strength, that is, as weaker than both the bullies and the control group. The bullies, on the other hand, were assessed as physically stronger, also when compared with the control boys, even if the result was not

TABLE 9

Incidence of Negative Deviations
among Whipping Boys (Wh), Control Boys (C), and Bullies (B).
Whipping Boys and Bullies from the First and Second
Solna Investigations Combined, Grade 6

| | Incidence of deviation | | | |
	Nondeviant	1–2 deviations	3 or more deviations	No. of boys
Wh	4	26	11	41
C	12	29	4	45
B	18	15	6	39
Total				125

Comparison	χ^2	p	C
Wh-C-B	17.04	< .01	.35
Wh-C	7.26	< .05	.28
B-C	5.65	< .10	.25
Wh-B	13.29	< .01	.38

significant in the second Solna investigation. Some results on this point are given in Table 10, where the boys are classified as negatively deviant (unusually weak), nondeviant, and positively deviant (unusually strong). These analyses have combined whipping boys and bullies from the two investigations. The most marked difference was found, as might be expected, between the whipping boys[1] and the bullies.

Thus, as regards physical strength, the whipping boys were more negatively deviant than the other groups, and it should be noted that these deviations were partly responsible for the differences in Table 9. When the incidence of negative deviations was calculated without including the variable physical strength, the tendency noticed in Table 9 was still present, but the difference between the whipping boys and the control group was not statistically significant, $p = .20$.

[1] In Table 10, one of the two whipping boys in the box for positive deviation (+), had been assessed as fluctuating between being whipping boy and bully.

It should also be mentioned that in the second Solna investigation, the whipping boys had significantly fewer positive deviations than the control group and the bullies. And the bullies had significantly more positive deviations than either the control group or the whipping boys in the first investigation. To some extent, this is a consequence of the fact that assessments of positive deviations for the most part concerned physical strength (and, to a limited extent, appearance).

In comparison, the well-adjusted group was, by and large, a plus group, with fewer negative deviations and also more positive deviations as regards strength and appearance. It is worth noting that, according to the teachers' assessments, there were no differences in physical strength between the bullies and the well-adjusted boys.

TABLE 10

Deviations with Regard to Physical Strength
among Whipping Boys (Wh), Control Boys (C), and Bullies (B).
Whipping Boys and Bullies from the
First and Second Solna Investigations Combined, Grade 6

	Physical strength			No. of boys
	—	0	+	
Wh	13	26	2	41
C	2	35	8	45
B	0	24	15	39
Total				125

+ Positive deviation, unusually strong.
0 Nondeviating, average.
— Negative deviation, unusually weak.

Comparison	χ^2	p	C
Wh-C-B	32.53	< .001	.45
Wh-C	12.84	< .01	.36
B-C	5.78	< .10	.25
Wh-B	22.99	< .001	.47

Comments

When evaluating these results, the question arises as to whether any bias in the method can have affected them. Here, it might be thought that the teachers, more or less consciously affected by stereotypic views of mobbing, perhaps tended to judge the whipping boys as more negatively deviant than they were (i.e., as perceived by their peers). Another possibility is that certain external deviations as regards, for instance, speech or facial expression in a whipping boy might have arisen as a consequence of protracted mobbing: The deviation did not exist when the mobbing began but was there when the assessment was made, that is, as a consequence of mobbing by other pupils, not as a possible cause or contributory factor. Both these circumstances suggest that the teachers' assessments of negative deviance in the whipping boys at any rate need not be considered as an underestimate with respect to the problems relevant here.

As regards the assessment of physical strength, it may be supposed that the evaluations made by the teachers were to some degree based on the outcome of fights and wrestling bouts he or she had witnessed, that is, on the ability of the boys to utilize their strength in fighting rather than on their actual strength. There are two points to be made in this context. In the first place, the bullies and the well-adjusted boys were assessed as much the same as regards physical strength (nonsignificant difference), and the well-adjusted boys were seldom mixed up in fights according to the peer ratings (p. 45). In the second place, certain follow-up data in the seventh grade for about half of the whipping boys, bullies, and well-adjusted boys in the first Solna investigation gave the following results: Peer ratings for ability in arm wrestling—probably a fairly pure indicator of physical strength—showed marked differences, the whipping boys ranking well below the approximately equal bullies and well-adjusted boys, $F(2, 26) = 5.84$, $p < .01$, epsilon $= .52$. Accordingly, it seems highly probable that as a group the whipping boys were physically weaker than is normal for their age.

According to the teachers, however, the whipping boys were not exceptionally small or fat. These assessments were, by the way, supported by the fact that there were no significant differences in height and weight between the whipping boys, the bullies, and a control group in the first Solna investigation, $F(2, 80) = .94$ and 1.14. The whipping boys were thus normal in height and weight. This suggests that at least some of the whipping boys—as many as 28 out of the 41 in Table 10 were not assessed as unusually weak—apparently either could not, would not, or dared not use their physical resources to defend themselves effectively. This circumstance is probably of great importance for an understanding of whipping boy problems and will be explored more thoroughly in Chapter 7.

The chief results so far can be summarized as follows: Considered as a group, the whipping boys showed some tendency to more negative deviations than the control boys. This tendency was very weak, however, except for physical strength, where the differences were marked. The bullies showed a tendency to fewer negative deviations and greater physical strength than both the control boys and the whipping boys. Other points will be taken up in the summarizing discussion.

ON BEING A FOREIGNER

The first Solna investigation, comprising approximately 300 boys, contained 28 boys of foreign origin, in the sense that either one or both of the biological parents of the boy were non-Swedish and/or the first language of the boy was not Swedish (according to information from the teachers). Many of these boys, however, had lived a long time, perhaps all their lives, in Sweden and spoke perfectly correct Swedish. For the present purposes, therefore, it was of greater interest to study the 14 boys who either because of their non-Swedish appearance or their inadequate grasp of the Swedish language might be regarded as deviant by their peers. I shall not make detailed analyses here but merely present some conclusions. The subject group is small, but it may be pointed out that similar results were obtained for the second Stockholm investigation ($n = 142$).

The analyses showed that the percentage of whipping boys among the 14 foreign boys (as defined above) was no higher than in the total number of subjects. While this group showed a slight tendency to greater adjustment problems, it should also be noted that several of these boys were assessed as well adjusted. It can be concluded that the foreign boys in the two investigations were not the target of mobbing to a greater degree than the other boys.

It is conceivable that foreign boys (or girls) when they first enter a class often get into a fairly difficult situation; the boys studied here had been in the class at least 6 months. Furthermore, it is possible that boys in the present subject group were unusually friendly to foreigners. Even if considerations of this nature point to limitations in the stated conclusion, the results obtained are in agreement with the conclusions reached by the school psychologists in Solna in a report on the adjustment of foreign children in Solna's primary schools (Goldinger & Mellis, 1970). It should also be stressed that the great majority of whipping boys in the Solna groups consisted of Swedish boys (nonforeigners). Thus, according to the results from these two investigations, whipping boy problems were not especially bound up with deviance in the form of foreign appearance or defective use of the Swedish language.

ON BEING A NEW BOY

Some data from the first Solna investigation provide an opportunity, though limited, to shed light on this problem. However, the results should be interpreted with caution. It should perhaps also be pointed out that this is not really a matter of external deviance. The problems involved, however, are related to those discussed in the last section.

Nine boys from other districts joined the classes in the first Solna investigation when these classes moved up to the seventh grade. None of these boys were assessed as whipping boys at the interviews with their teachers 8 or 9 months later.

Fourteen boys changed classes in moving from the sixth to the seventh grade. Ten of these had not been assessed as whipping boys when they were in the sixth grade. None of them were assessed as whipping boys in grade 7. Thus none of the 19 boys (9 + 10) entering new classes at the seventh-grade stage became whipping boys according to the teachers' assessments.

This suggests that being a new boy does not in itself increase the risk of becoming a whipping boy, at any rate not for longer periods of time.

SUMMARIZING DISCUSSION

In contrast to what has been commonly assumed, the whipping boys were only marginally more deviant in external characteristics than boys in general. On the whole, the whipping boys were not fatter, had no more physical handicaps, and no more peculiar clothes than the other boys. Nor was there a higher percentage of foreign boys among the whipping boys than in the subject group as a whole. Accordingly, it can be concluded that external deviations of the kind mentioned seem to play a much smaller role for the appearance of whipping boy problems than has usually been believed.

In one external characteristic, however, there were noticeable differences between the groups. This characteristic is physical strength, actually a deviation of a very different type from those usually considered. The whipping boys were clearly physically weaker than the control boys, while the bullies were assessed as stronger than the control boys (tendency) and much stronger than the whipping boys. It should be noted, however, that even if the distributions in Table 10 were fairly different, a number of the whipping boys as well as the bullies were rated as average in physical strength. This fact and the circumstance that the well-adjusted, nonaggressive boys were assessed as approximately as strong as the bullies suggest that other factors, including factors of a psychological character, played a crucial part in determining whether whipping boy/bully problems would arise. Such factors will be considered in the next chapter.

In this connection, it is worth emphasizing that the bullies were by and large a plus group as regards external characteristics. This fact may conflict with the fairly common view, for example, of bullies being fat—like whipping boys—or of having physical defects for which they try to compensate. This type of bully certainly occurs, as the descriptions of some of the boys in the investigations also showed, but as a whole the bullies had more positive and fewer negative deviations than the boys in the other groups.

The reasons why external deviations have attracted so much attention in the general debate are certainly many and complex. I shall confine myself to commenting on one possible reason. In trying to understand a problem such as mobbing, it is perhaps natural to notice in the first place special external features or stimuli in the victims: Do whipping boys deviate in their external appearance as compared with others? As evident from Table 9 (p. 84), there were a lot of external deviations in the whipping boys. However, examination of the data for the control group in the same table reveals that nearly all the boys were "deviant" with respect to some external characteristic. Approximately 75% of the randomly selected boys were assessed as deviating on one or more points. Accordingly, those looking for deviance as an explanation of whipping boy problems can easily find support for their hypothesis—so long as they do not make comparisons with what is common in a randomly selected control group.

On the basis of the results reported in this chapter, it can be maintained that external deviations have been much over-emphasized in the Swedish debate on mobbing, with the exception of physical strength, which has scarcely been discussed at all. This conclusion does not deny that certain forms of external deviance may constitute a *risk factor* that to some extent increases the probability of an individual boy becoming a whipping boy. A number of other factors, however, are of far greater significance in determining whether a boy will actually become a whipping boy or not. One of these factors, but by no means the only one, is physical strength.

The main points in this chapter can be summarized as follows.

- The whipping boys were only marginally more deviant in external characteristics than randomly selected control boys.
- Only as regards physical strength were the whipping boys clearly more deviating (weaker) than the control boys.
- The bullies had fewer negative and more positive deviations than the control boys (tendency) and, in particular, than the whipping boys.

- According to the teachers' assessments, external deviance was very common. External deviations of one kind or another appeared in approximately 75% of the boys in the control group.
- The results obtained suggest that the importance of external deviations for the appearance of whipping boy problems has been much exaggerated in the public debate (with the exception of physical strength, which has scarcely been discussed in this context). External deviations can perhaps be regarded as a risk factor but of rather limited significance.

7

PSYCHOLOGICAL AND OTHER CHARACTERISTICS OF WHIPPING BOYS AND BULLIES

In this chapter, whipping boys and bullies will be looked at more closely as regards the characteristics included in Sector C of the theory sketch, that is, behavioral characteristics, psychological characteristics, and those reflecting the attitude or behavior of others toward a boy. A variety of tests and methods have been used, and only the main results will be reported here. As a rule, these results have been confirmed in several different samples and by means of somewhat different methods.

In addition, some data about the social background of the boys (Sector D) will be given. In the final section of the chapter, the 3-year follow-up data on four rating variables will be presented, providing information about the stability over time of some of the characteristics under study.

For the reader's convenience, the results will be summarized at the end of each section instead of at the end of the chapter.

THE PEER RATINGS

A brief presentation of the peer ratings in the first Solna investigation was given in Chapter 4—see, in particular, Figure 2 and Table 3 and the comments on them. Here, the results will be summarized and commented on further. The intercorrelations among the peer-rated variables are presented in the final section of the chapter (Table 15).

According to the peer ratings, the bullies were far more aggressive than the control boys and the whipping boys. These results were obtained for all three variables concerning aggressive behavior—Start Fights, Verbal Protest, and Tease. No difference appeared between the bullies and the control group as regards the variable Popularity, a circumstance worth emphasizing. Nor was there a difference in the Aggression Target variable. The bullies were thus no more often attacked by other boys than were boys in general. Their mean value was even somewhat lower than that of the control boys (though not statistically significant).

As expected, the whipping boys had high scores on the variable Aggression Target and were clearly less popular with their peers than either the control group or the bullies. They were also rated as very nonaggressive, and this was also the case for the variable Tease. It is a fairly common belief that a whipping boy has a teasing manner himself and that he, perhaps unconsciously, tries to irritate others in order to attract attention, to gain contact with others, or even to satisfy some kind of self-destructive (masochistic) tendencies. The peer ratings and the teacher descriptions provide grounds for thinking that such mechanisms might be present in two or three of the whipping boys, but the large majority of them clearly did not have a teasing manner according to their peers (see also p. 122). Consequently, the results obtained do not support the stated belief.

As Figure 2 (p. 45) shows, the well-adjusted boys had low values on all variables except Popularity.

It should be recalled that very similar results to those presented above were obtained in the two Stockholm investigations (see p. 46). This fact lends additional generality to the findings reported.

In the first Solna investigation, the degree of a boy's popularity could also be studied by means of sociometric choices. As the final question in the inventory Our Class, each boy was asked to choose the four boys in the class with whom he would prefer to spend the breaks (i.e., only positive choices).

The girls were asked to choose the two boys in the class they liked best. The results for the boys' choices agreed well with those for the variable Popularity. On the average, the whipping boys were chosen least frequently, the bullies were next, then the control boys, and finally the well-adjusted boys (F for one of the sociometric indexes[1] $= 17.27$, $p < .0001$, $df = 3$, 108, epsilon $= .5$). Measured in this way, the bullies were less popular than the control boys, $p < .05$, but they were clearly more popular than the whipping boys, $p < .01$. Many of the whipping boys were not chosen at all in spite of the fact that each boy had as many as four choices. Only one of the bullies was not chosen at all. The others were usually chosen by two or three boys, which indicates that they were liked by or had support from at least some boys in the class. In comparison, the control boys were chosen by three or four boys, as a rule.

A point of interest is that the bullies were better liked by the girls than by the control boys (though not significantly, $p = .10$) but, in agreement with the boys' choices, the well-adjusted boys were the most popular of the four groups. The popularity of the whipping boys was no greater with the girls than with the boys.

From a methodological point of view, it is worth emphasizing that there was a correlation of .70 between the variable Popularity and the sociometric variable *number of times chosen* (the boys' choices) for the sample as a whole ($n = 247$). This means that these two measures of popularity, arrived at in two entirely different ways, agreed very well with each other. In addition, a number of boys were found who were not very popular with their peers, but who were still not whipping boys according to the teacher assessments. In other words, lack of popularity, as measured by sociometric choices or by other means, is obviously not synonymous with being a whipping boy. There are certainly outsiders of various kinds who may be chosen few times or not at all in a sociometric investigation but who, by and large, are content with or accept their situation; and they are not the target of other boys' attacks. It is also probable

---

[1] Several indexes were constructed taking into account the number of choosers and the number of boys to choose among.

that a bully would occasionally get included among a group of "whipping boys," if degree of popularity were the only selection criterion. Such circumstances point to the dangers of defining a whipping boy (only) on the basis of lack of popularity.

Some of the main points in this section may be summarized as follows.

- According to their peers, the whipping boys were non-aggressive, they were often the target of aggression from others, and they were unpopular among both boys and girls.
- The fairly common belief that whipping boys usually have a teasing manner was not confirmed by the data.
- The bullies were very aggressive and relatively popular among both boys and girls. The bullies were thus not isolated but were liked or supported as a rule by two or three boys in the class. They were seldom the target of other boys' aggression.
- The well-adjusted boys, like the whipping boys, were nonaggressive, but in contrast to the whipping boys, they were very popular among both girls and boys. They were seldom the target of attack from others.

DATA FROM THE BOYS AND THEIR MOTHERS

In the previous section, the results on the peer rating variables were presented. The following two sections will deal with data provided by the boys themselves (self-reports) and by their mothers (in the first Solna investigation). First, however, a summary description will follow of the methods and samples used (see also Chapter 3).

Methods

A

A special questioning technique, known as the *Q* sort, was employed on the three special groups from the first Solna investigation—21 whipping boys, 22 well-adjusted boys, and 21 bullies. A total of 57 statements were written on as many small cards, and the boy was asked to grade how well each statement applied to him (e.g., "I prefer to get out of the way when somebody is picking on me"; "Generally I am fairly sure of myself"). The boy had to place the 57 items in seven different piles representing the following categories: applies very well to me, applies well to me, applies fairly well to me, applies neither well nor poorly to me, applies fairly poorly to me, applies poorly to me, applies very poorly to me. The subject had to follow a forced distribution insofar as he had to put at least 6 and no more than 10 cards in each pile. This distributional form was chosen after preliminary experimentation. The Q sorts were all administered individually by the same male psychologist. A Q sort took about an hour. Each statement was scored from 7 (applies very well to me) to 1 (applies very poorly to me).

The mothers of the boys in these groups ($n = 62$; 2 mothers refused to participate) also carried out the same Q sort with regard to their sons. Each mother thus had to decide how well each of the statements applied to her son. The wording of the statements was the same as for the boys except that the "I" form was exchanged for the third person, for example, "I prefer to get out of the way when somebody is picking on me" was changed to "He prefers to get out of the way when somebody is picking on him." Corresponding changes were made for the seven categories or piles: applies very well to him (my son), and so on.

With regard to content, the items of the Q sort can be roughly divided into five main areas: (1) aggression and violence—19 items, (2) anxiety—7 items, (3) self-esteem—9 items, (4) identification—10 items, and (5) closeness to parents—8 items. In addition, two items relating to conformity and two filler items were included (see Appendix). The main areas were selected on the basis of theoretical considerations of the nature of whipping boy/bully problems. In some analyses, the average value for all the items belonging to a particular area (with the exception of identification) is calculated for each individual; the resulting composite scales will be referred to as *a priori dimensions*. As evident from the foregoing, these dimensions, which may partially overlap, have not been isolated by means of statistical dimensional analysis. However, the results of such an analysis will be briefly described in a following section concerning the second Solna investigation.

The Q-sort method is often considered to have certain advantages over a conventional inventory in that it forces the subject to make more careful judgments. Employment of a forced distribution is also thought to counteract certain response biases (sets), for instance, the tendency of some subjects to choose a given alternative more or less independently of the content of the statement or question. On the other hand, in the Q-sort method, the subject must make judgments involving comparisons of how well a large number of statements apply to him (or to her son), and this may be a more difficult task than answering questions in an inventory, especially for younger subjects (see, e.g., Block, 1961; or Cronbach, 1970, for general information about the Q-sort method).

In the following analyses, somewhat more weight will be placed on the mothers' Q sorts. There are two reasons for this. In the first place, the mothers' descriptions of their boys (through the Q sort) were found to distinguish between the three groups for more of the statements than the boys' own Q sorts. In all, there were significant differences between the groups for 35 of the 55 statements (excluding the 2 filler items) according to the mothers' sorts, as opposed to 20 statements for the boys' sorts (using a .10 significance level, which may be justifiable since many differences were expected on the basis of a priori considerations; with a .05 significance level, the corresponding figures were 28 and 15). There was, however, considerable agreement as to the results obtained: 17 of the 20 statements that distinguished between the groups according to the boys' sorts also differentiated the groups according to the sorts made by the mothers. But there were 18 additional statements that differentiated the groups only according to the mothers' sorts, though a tendency in the same direction could often be found in the boys' sorts. These results suggest that the mothers' descriptions of their boys agreed, in the main, with the boys' own descriptions, but that the mothers' descriptions were more accurate. It may be that the boys could not or would not give as "correct" descriptions of themselves as their mothers gave.

In the second place, the mothers' descriptions in the area of aggression showed somewhat greater validity than those of the boys. When the a priori scale for the area of aggression and violence (19 items) was correlated with the peer-rated variables Start Fights, Verbal Protest, and Tease, consistently higher values were obtained for the mothers' descriptions: The correlation coefficients were .67, .62, and .62 ($n = 62$) against the boys' .54, .47, and .53 ($n = 64$). These results, too, support the assumption that the mothers' descriptions of the boys were, on the whole, more "correct" than the boys' descriptions of themselves. In addition, these results provide general support for the validity of the descriptions given by the mothers as well as by the boys, at least in the area of aggression.

B

The 57 items of the Q sort were administered to the boys in the second Solna investigation (grade 6) in the form of a conventional inventory. The seven response alternatives employed in the individual administration, from "applies very well to me" (scored 7) to "applies very poorly to me" (scored 1), were also used in the inventory. The inventory was group-administered to the boys in each of the participating classes (19 classes). This instrument will be called the Q inventory in the following discussion.

An image factor analysis (Jöreskog, 1963) was carried out on the Q-inventory data from all the boys in ordinary classes ($n = 197$, data were lacking on 6 subjects, and 14 boys were in special classes). Eight factors were extracted (with eigenvalues greater than 1.00) and orthogonally rotated, according to the varimax criterion (Kaiser, 1959). In order to examine the degree of reliability or invariance of the solution obtained (Armstrong & Soelberg, 1968), the total subject group was randomly split into two subgroups of equal size ($n_1 = 99$, $n_2 = 98$), and identical factor analyses were performed within each subgroup. The four factors with the largest eigenvalues showed very similar factorial structure in the two samples, and these factors were tentatively interpreted as follows. The largest factor (I) comprising 12 items chiefly from the a priori areas of anxiety, self-esteem, and identification seemed primarily to reflect feelings of maladjustment and inadequacy (the items constituting the different factor variables and their respective factor loadings are shown in the Appendix). Eleven items defined factor II, which was called aggression. The third factor (III) comprised 10 items concerned with self-confidence, independence, and perhaps toughness. Factor IV primarily contained items suggesting a close, positive, trustful contact with the parents and with adults in general. This factor variable comprising 10 items was called closeness to parents. In all, 43 of the 55 items of the Q inventory were included in the four factors, with each item having a factor loading of .37 or higher. A boy's score on a factor variable was obtained by averaging his scores on the individual items defining that particular factor.

The internal consistency reliability values (alpha coefficients) of the four factor variables were .85 (I), .82 (II), .77 (III), and .81 (IV), respectively.

As to the validity of the factor scales, the following may be reported. In the second Solna investigation, peer ratings were collected for the variables Start Fights, Verbal Protest, Tease, Aggression Target, and Popularity. In eight classes ($n = 105$), all the boys in each class rated all the other boys in the class, the average number of raters being 13. The reliabilities of the composite ratings (the average of all the ratings for a boy on a particular variable) can be estimated to lie between .85 and .95 for these five variables (see Olweus, 1977a). As expected, there were substantial positive correlations between the factor variable aggression (II) and the aggressive peer-rated variables, the coefficients being .47, .49, and .46 with Start Fights, Verbal Protest, and Tease, respectively. These peer-rated variables were also positively correlated with the factor variable self-confidence (toughness, III), the coefficients being .42, .42, and .46. The sum of the two factor variables II and III correlated .61 with the sum of the three aggressive peer-rated variables. These results are in agreement with what has been reported earlier for similar inventory variables and age groups (see Olweus, 1973a, 1975). Moreover, the first factor variable, feelings of maladjustment and inadequacy, correlated .31 with the peer variable Aggression Target and −.29 with Popularity. These results, which imply that boys who felt maladjusted, anxious, and inadequate tended to be less popular and more often the target of other boys' aggression, appear quite reasonable. Finally, there was a correlation of $-.25$ between the factor variable closeness to parents (and other adults, IV) and the peer-rated tendency to answer back and protest against a criticizing teacher (Verbal Protest), which also makes sense.

When evaluating these results, it should be noted that validity coefficients of the order of .45-.60 (uncorrected for attenuation), which were obtained for the second and third factor variables (and their sum), are fairly unusual in psychological research. Furthermore, as regards the remaining factor variables (I and IV), there is no reason to expect high and direct correspondence with the peer-rated variables mentioned. The coefficients reported, however, appear very reasonable, and it may be generally concluded that the results obtained provide strong support for the validity of the Q inventory and the factor scales, in particular with respect to the aggressive motive area.

The subject groups for which data from the Q inventory will be reported in the following sections consisted of 14 whipping boys,[2] 17 bullies, and 59 control boys randomly selected from the rest of the boys. These whipping boys and bullies may be considered the most marked ones of their kind in the 19 classes studied.

In order not to make reading too cumbersome, data on individual items will not be reported for these groups. It should be noted, however, that on all essential points the trends found in the first Solna investigation were confirmed and were often strengthened in the second Solna study. Here results will be presented only for the a priori dimensions and the four factor scales.

C

The boys' attitude to violence and aggression will also be highlighted by means of data from the second Stockholm investigation (see p. 29). In this study, the boys were tested with a specially constructed attitude form called Aggressive

---

[2] Only what were called passive whipping boys were included in this group. Q-inventory data were lacking on one whipping boy and one control boy.

Attitude, comprising 17 statements (each scored from 6 to 1) from four a priori areas (and some fillers). The boys in this study were also administered a self-evaluation form and a semantic differential. The self-evaluation form contained 30 statements (each scored from 6 to 1) designed to measure certain aspects of the boys' attitude toward themselves (e.g., anxiety), to their situation (e.g., contact with parents), and to schoolwork. The semantic differential consisted of 15 adjective pairs such as: anxious-bold, strong-weak, quick-slow (each scale scored from 9 to 1). This technique, too, aimed at reflecting certain aspects of the boys' self-evaluation—to what extent they usually had a positive or negative attitude toward themselves.

Data were obtained from 10 whipping boys, 11 bullies, and 60 control boys.

RELATION TO AGGRESSION AND VIOLENCE

Results

Generally, there were many and very marked differences between the groups within the aggressive area. The Q sort descriptions given by the boys themselves and by their mothers agreed well, and for no less than 12 of the 19 statements, the group differences were significant (.10 significance level) according to both boys and mothers. Only two statements failed to yield reliable differences between the groups in either the mothers' or the boys' Q sorts. Five statements differentiated the groups only according to the mothers.

In the second Solna investigation, 16 out of the 19 items pertaining to aggression and violence differentiated the whipping boys, the bullies, and the control boys (.10 significance level). The results for the a priori dimension aggression and violence are presented in Table 11, for the first as well as the second Solna investigations. Figure 3 shows the results on the factor variable aggression for the second Solna investigation. The table and the figure clearly demonstrate that the differences between the groups were very pronounced.

A more detailed picture of the results is obtained by examination of Table 12, which presents data on a selection of

TABLE 11

Mean Values, *F* and *t* Tests on Four A Priori Dimensions for
Whipping Boys (Wh), Well-Adjusted Boys (A), Bullies (B), and
Control Boys (C) from the First and the Second Solna Investigations.
Score 7 = Applies Very Well, Score 1 = Applies Very Poorly.

Dimension and statistic	Boys' Q sort	Mothers' Q sort	Boys' Q inventory
Aggression and violence (19 items)	Wh = 3.39 A = 3.35 B = 4.39	Wh = 3.64 A = 3.33 B = 4.83	Wh = 3.36 C = 3.83 B = 4.99
F	16.15	31.72	21.47
p	< .0001	< .0001	< .0001
t[a]	B > Wh = A	B > Wh = A	B > C > Wh
epsilon	.57	.71	.56
Anxiety (7 items)	Wh = 3.46 A = 2.92 B = 3.24	Wh = 3.69 A = 3.20 B = 2.76	Wh = 4.00 C = 3.23 B = 2.51
F	1.92	5.40	14.78
p	n.s.	< .01	< .0001
t		Wh > A = B	Wh > C > B
epsilon		.36	.49
Self-esteem (negative, 9 items)	Wh = 2.75 A = 2.13 B = 2.68	Wh = 3.28 A = 2.12 B = 2.71	Wh = 3.39 C = 2.68 B = 2.51
F	3.34	7.15	5.85
p	< .05	< .005	< .005
t	Wh = B > A	Wh > B > A	Wh > C = B
epsilon	.26	.41	.31
Closeness to parents (8 items)	Wh = 4.19 A = 4.39 B = 3.98	Wh = 4.53 A = 4.72 B = 4.17	Wh = 4.25 C = 3.89 B = 3.22
F	1.47	3.57	4.73
p	n.s.	< .05	< .05
t		A = Wh > B	Wh = C > B
epsilon		.28	.28

Number of subjects

Boy's Q sort	Mother's Q sort	Boys' Q inventory
Wh = 21	Wh = 20	Wh = 14
A = 22	A = 21	A = 59
B = 21	B = 21	B = 17

[a]Two-tailed tests and a .05 significance level were used.

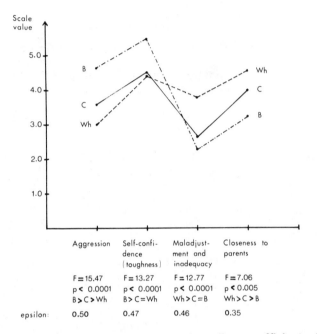

	Aggression	Self-confidence (toughness)	Maladjustment and inadequacy	Closeness to parents
	$F = 15.47$	$F = 13.27$	$F = 12.77$	$F = 7.06$
	$p < 0.0001$	$p < 0.0001$	$p < 0.0001$	$p < 0.005$
	B > C > Wh	B > C = Wh	Wh > C = B	Wh > C > B
epsilon:	0.50	0.47	0.46	0.35

FIGURE 3. Mean values, F values, and epsilon coefficients for comparisons between whipping boys (Wh, $n = 14$), control boys (C, $n = 59$), and bullies (B, $n = 17$) on the factor dimensions derived in the second Solna investigation.

individual items from the first Solna investigation. It should be noted, however, that the conclusions to be drawn are also based on other items not included in the table and on the results from the second Solna study.

The first statement in Table 12 is concerned with the intensity of the boys' inner aggressive reactions. The bullies thus became angry more easily than the whipping boys and the well-adjusted boys. The results suggest that the bullies had a lower threshold for aggressive reactions or were more irascible.

The second statement concerns the boys' tendency to react with verbally aggressive behavior to disappointment (frustration) occasioned by a teacher. Also on this point, the bullies showed a greater propensity to react aggressively than did the other groups.

The third and fourth statements bear on the degree of control or inhibition of aggressive feelings and tendencies (impulse control). Both the whipping boys and the well-adjusted

TABLE 12

Comparison of Whipping Boys (Wh), Well-Adjusted Boys (A), and Bullies (B)
for a Selection of Statements from the A Priori Area
of Aggression and Violence. From the Mothers' and Boys'
Q sorts in the First Solna Investigation (62 Mothers, 64 Boys).
Score 7 = Applies Very Well, Score 1 = Applies Very Poorly.

Statement		Mean Value			F	p	epsilon	t test[a]
		Wh	A	B				
1. I get angry with other people easily (41).[b]	Mothers	3.80	2.86	4.95	7.23	< .005	.41	B > Wh = A
	Boys	3.52	2.76	4.73	7.62	< .001	.42	B > Wh = A
2. If a teacher has promised we'll have some fun but then changes his mind, I protest strongly (39).	Mothers	4.20	4.43	6.09	7.80	< .001	.43	B > A = Wh
	Boys	3.24	4.67	6.00	12.85	< .001	.52	B > A > Wh
3. If I get angry, I usually don't show it (37).	Mothers	3.10	3.48	1.90	6.46	< .005	.39	B < Wh = A
	Boys	4.10	4.24	3.27	1.64	= .20		
4. I think it is better to be quiet than to make a fuss if somebody is unpleasant (18).	Mothers	4.45	5.00	2.52	14.90	< .001	.56	B < Wh = A
	Boys	5.24	4.86	3.32	10.24	< .001	.48	B < Wh = A
5. I think fighting is silly (55).	Mothers	5.80	6.00	3.52	16.83	< .001	.59	B < Wh = A
	Boys	5.67	6.29	4.23	9.25	< .001	.46	B < Wh = A
6. I often think it is fun to make trouble (6).	Mothers	3.70	3.33	5.48	7.43	< .005	.42	B > Wh = A
	Boys	3.09	3.29	5.18	13.59	< .001	.53	B > Wh = A
7. I think a boy should be able to take a few knocks (32).	Mothers	3.70	4.90	5.48	9.77	< .001	.47	B = A > Wh
	Boys	4.71	5.33	5.54	.97	n.s.		

[a] Two-tailed t tests and a .05 significance level were used.
[b] The number in parenthesis refers to the order in which the statements were presented in the Q sort.

boys were characterized by relatively strong control, whereas the bullies expressed aggressive impulses more freely. Taking into account the results for the first statement, it can be concluded that the aggressive tendencies of the bullies were very likely not only of greater intensity, but also more weakly controlled than those of the whipping boys and the well-adjusted boy.

The fifth and sixth statements reflect the degree of positive (or negative) attitude to physical aggression and making trouble more generally. The attitude of both the whipping boys and the well-adjusted boys was negative, while the bullies showed a more positive attitude.

The final statement revealed a difference between the whipping boys and the well-adjusted boys, according to the mothers' descriptions; the difference between the well-adjusted boys and the bullies was smaller and not significant. The results for the boys' Q sorts were in the same direction but were far from significant. Thus, according to the mothers, the well-adjusted boys considered, to a greater degree than the whipping boys, that boys should be able to take a few knocks. This result suggests a gentler, perhaps weaker, attitude in the whipping boys (their mothers) to what a "boy's role" implies or demands. The well-adjusted boys and the bullies even more appeared to think that a "real boy" normally should be able to take a few knocks—it is natural in the life of a boy. However, such a view cannot be interpreted as a positive attitude to violence. This is shown by the well-adjusted boys' answers to the previous statements.

In this connection, the results for the second statement should be noted once more. This item concerns the degree to which the boy protests if a teacher promises that the class will have some fun but then changes his mind. Even here, where opposition to the teacher may seem reasonably justified, the whipping boys were more restrained than the well-adjusted boys. Thus the whipping boys and the well-adjusted boys manifested some interesting differences in spite of the fact that by and large they had fairly similar scores in the area of aggression.

Before I comment on these results, Table 13 should also be examined. It shows the results for three typical statements from the Aggressive Attitude form used in the second Stockholm

TABLE 13

Comparison of Whipping Boys (Wh), Bullies (B) and Control Boys (C)
for a Selection of Statements from the Aggressive Area. From the Form
Aggressive Attitude Used in the Second Stockholm Investigation
(Data from 9 Whipping Boys, 10 Bullies, and 59 Control Boys).
Score 6 = Applies Exactly, Score 1 = Does not Apply at All

| Statement | Mean value | | | F | p | epsilon | t test[a] |
	Wh	C	B				
Fighting is often the best way to solve conflicts	2.78	2.19	3.70	4.95	< .01	.31	B > Wh = C
I would like to become a boxer	1.22	1.86	3.40	6.16	< .005	.34	B > C = Wh
I think one should be nice to those who are younger and weaker	4.56	4.51	3.20	5.52	< .01	.32	B < C = Wh

[a]Two-tailed tests and a .05 significance level were used.

investigation. The bullies' generally positive attitude to violence
and violent means shows up clearly here. The bullies, to a
reliably greater degree than the control boys and the whipping
boys, agreed with the statements that fighting is the best way to
solve conflicts, and that he (the respondent) would like to
become a boxer. The bullies also had a more negative attitude to
"those who are younger and weaker." In all four a priori areas,
positive attitude to physical violence, being "well brought up,"
aggression toward adults, and negative attitude to deviants, the
bullies were distinguished by a more aggressive or hostile attitude. The differences were highly significant on the sum variables for the first two areas.

Comments

In its main outlines, the picture emerging from these results
is very clear. The bullies, in their own eyes as well as in the eyes
of their mothers, were far more aggressive than the whipping
boys, the well-adjusted boys, and the control boys. This general
conclusion agrees very well with the results from the peer
ratings. However, the boys' self-reports and the mothers' Q-sort
descriptions contained information that gives depth and detail to

the picture of the boys' reactions and behavior in the aggressive motive area.

The bullies were distinguished both by their more irascible temperaments or stronger aggressive tendencies and their weaker control, if such tendencies were activated: They habitually behaved more aggressively and restrained themselves less when angry or provoked. Furthermore, they showed a distinctly more positive attitude to violence and violent means. It may be maintained that the bullies were characterized by a spirit of violence.

For many of the statements, there were only small and nonsignificant differences between the whipping boys and the well-adjusted boys. These groups of boys were characterized by a "normal" temperament, a relatively strong control of aggressive tendencies when activated, and a negative attitude to violence and violent means. Both the whipping boys and the well-adjusted boys could be considered generally nonaggressive, in behavior as well as in attitude. These similarities, however, should not overshadow the differences that the analyses also revealed: As compared with the whipping boys, the well-adjusted boys were more prone to protest against a frustrating teacher, and they felt to a greater degree that boys should be able to take a few knocks (according to their mothers). These results suggest that the nonaggressive behavior of the whipping boys originated from motives other than those of the well-adjusted boys. It is possible that the whipping boys either couldn't or didn't dare to be aggressive even in situations where some form of aggressive or assertive behavior might have been regarded as justified. I shall return to this point in a later section.

In concluding this section, it should be generally emphasized that on all essential points, concordant results were obtained in three different samples (or four, if the mothers are regarded as a separate sample) and with somewhat different methods. This should lend additional credence to the conclusions drawn.

The main results from this section may be summarized as follows.

- According to the descriptions given by the boys themselves and by their mothers, there were many and very

marked differences between the boys in the aggressive
motive area.

- The bullies were distinguished by a generally aggressive
reaction pattern and a clearly more positive attitude to
violence and violent means.
- The whipping boys and the well-adjusted boys resembled
each other in being nonaggressive in behavior and attitudes. Certain results, however, suggested that the motivation behind the generally nonaggressive behavior was
different for these two categories of boys.

ANXIETY, SELF-ESTEEM, AND OTHER AREAS

Results

Of the seven statements in the a priori dimension of anxiety,
four showed reliable group differences (.10 significance level)
according to the mothers' Q sorts (the first Solna investigation).
The boys' Q sorts revealed no significant differences, but for
two of the statements there was a clear tendency in the same
direction as indicated by the mothers. On the composite scale (7
items), significant differences, $p < .01$ (Table 11), were found for
the mothers' Q sorts. As expected, the whipping boys were more
anxious and apprehensive than both the well-adjusted boys and
the bullies (examples of differentiating statements: "I am usually
fairly brave," $F = 4.13$, $p < .05$; "I find it difficult to speak up
in class," $F = 4.40$, $p < .05$). As a rule, the differences between
the bullies and the well-adjusted boys were insignificant.

The results from the second Solna investigation were generally consistent with those just reported. Four of the items
reflecting the area of anxiety differentiated the groups according
to the boys' self-reports (through the Q inventory). As is evident
from Table 11 (under "Boys' Q inventory"), the differences
were marked, the whipping boys being more anxious than the
control boys, who in turn were more anxious than the bullies.

The self-evaluation form used in the second Stockholm
investigation showed that the whipping boys were more afraid
that something unpleasant might happen to them than were the
control boys, whereas the bullies were found to be less afraid

than the control boys. According to the semantic differential, the whipping boys saw themselves as more nervous than the control boys and especially the bullies. All the differences mentioned were significant at the .05 or .01 level.

The step from anxiety to negative self-esteem does not seem long. Of the nine statements that can be assumed to reflect a negative (or positive) view of oneself and one's own situation, eight differentiated the groups significantly according to either the mothers' or the boys' Q sorts (the first Solna investigation). Two items distinguished among the groups according to both mothers' and boys' sorts, while six distinguished among them only according to the mothers. Among other things, the whipping boys were less sure of themselves and found their situation difficult and troublesome to a greater extent than either one of the other groups. Even if the differences on several of the individual statements were not very marked, the composite scale (9 items) for the mothers' Q sorts showed clear results: The whipping boys had a generally more negative or less positive attitude toward themselves (lower self-esteem) than the bullies, and these in their turn were less positive about themselves than the well-adjusted boys, $F = 7.15, p < .005$ (see Table 11). The corresponding variable for the boys' sorts did not show any difference between the whipping boys and the bullies, but the well-adjusted boys were found to evaluate themselves more positively, $F = 3.34, p < .05$.

No less than seven of the nine items pertaining to the a priori area of self-esteem differentiated the groups (.10 significance level) in the second Solna investigation. As shown in Table 11 (under "Boys' Q inventory"), the whipping boys were characterized by a less positive view of themselves than the control boys and the bullies.

On the semantic differential (the second Stockholm investigation), the bullies gave on the whole a more positive evaluation of themselves than the control boys and the whipping boys (the bullies considered themselves wiser, faster, less weak, etc.). The differences between the whipping boys and the control boys were not very pronounced, but the trend was clearly in the direction of a more negative self-evaluation by the whipping boys.

At this point, it is appropriate to examine the results on the factor variables feelings of maladjustment and inadequacy (I), and self-confidence (toughness, III), which were isolated in the second Solna investigation. These two factor dimensions consisted of items belonging chiefly to the a priori areas of self-esteem and anxiety (the first dimension also contained items relating to identification, and the second dimension items relating to aggression). The findings on these dimensions were generally consistent with what has been reported above. As is evident from Figure 3, the whipping boys felt much more maladjusted, anxious, and inadequate than the control boys and the bullies. The difference between the control boys and the bullies was not significant. As regards self-confidence (independence and toughness), the bullies were found to have much higher values than the other two groups. There was a small and insignificant difference between the control boys and the whipping boys on this variable.

The a priori area identification contained ten somewhat heterogeneous statements. Four of these differentiated the groups according to the mothers' and/or the boys' Q sorts (.10 significance level, the first Solna investigation). According to the mothers, the whipping boys would like to "change many things about themselves" to a greater extent than the bullies and the well-adjusted boys, $F = 5.95$, $p < .005$. Two of the statements concerned relations with the father, and here the mothers' and the boys' descriptions revealed the same tendency: The bullies had less positive attitudes toward their fathers than both the other groups.[3] The differences between the whipping boys and the well-adjusted boys were not significant for these statements. As many as six items from the identification area differentiated among the groups in the second Solna investigation (.10 significance level), and the trends manifested in the first Solna investigation were generally confirmed and strengthened. Since the statements pertaining to identification relations were

---

[3] The statements were: (1) "When I grow up I want to be like my father." Mothers: $F = 4.07$, $p < .05$; Boys: $F = 3.62$, $p < .05$). (2) "I often have fun with my father." Mothers: $F = 3.18$, $p < .05$; Boys: $F = 1.82$, $p = .17$, not significant).

somewhat heterogeneous, it did not seem meaningful to form a composite scale of all the ten statements.

In the a priori area closeness to parents (and other adults, IV), four of the eight statements differentiated among the groups according to the boys' and/or the mothers' Q sorts (.10 significance level). The results could be interpreted as indicating that the bullies had less close contact with their parents than the whipping boys and the well-adjusted boys (Examples: "I nearly always tell my mother what I have been doing." Boys: $F = 2.56$, $p = .08$; Mothers: $F = 2.75, p = .07$. "I like to have a grown-up around." Mothers: $F = 5.19, p < .01$. The composite scale (8 items) showed the same tendency, the results being significant for the mothers' descriptions (see Table 11).

Similar though somewhat more accentuated differences were obtained in the second Solna investigation. Three out of eight statements differentiated among the group (.10 significance level), and on the composite scale the bullies were clearly different from the whipping boys and the well-adjusted boys (see Table 11). Even more marked differences were obtained on the factor IV dimension closeness to parents (containing 10 items coming largely from the a priori area). On this scale, the whipping boys were significantly separated from the control boys, who in turn were reliably differentiated from the bullies (see Figure 3).

The assumption that the bullies had less positive contact with or a more negative attitude to their parents also received support from the answers to the statement "I have wanted to run away from home several times." In their Q sorts, the bullies agreed with this statement to a greater extent than the other groups, $F = 2.77, p = .07$. In the Stockholm investigation, where the same statement was part of the self-evaluation form, the tendency was the same: The bullies agreed with the statement to a greater degree than the whipping boys and the control boys, but the difference was not significant, $p = .22$. The self-evaluation form also contained two other statements of interest. The statement "Nobody at home cares much for me" was accepted by the bullies to a greater extent than by the boys in the other two groups, $F = 3.98, p < .05$. Furthermore, the bullies considered the statement "My parents and I usually get along very well together" less applicable than did the other two groups. The difference was not significant, however, $p = .15$.

In the Q sort and the Q inventory, there were also two items presumably relating to conformity. No systematic trends could be detected for these items, and the differences on the sum of them were small and not significant in both the first (boys and mothers) and the second Solna investigations.

Since results from the self-evaluation form and the semantic differential have been reported only on selected points, one may ask whether these instruments also manifested tendencies that did not agree with the findings from the Q data. It is therefore important to point out that no systematic group differences were found on these instruments that conflicted with the trends derived from the Q sorts and the Q inventory. On only one point were results obtained that deserve some comment. These results will be taken up in the discussion of the anxiety area for the bullies.

Comments

First, it should be generally emphasized that there were also many important differences between the groups in areas other than aggression and violence, particularly according to the mothers' Q sorts and the boys' self-descriptions in the Q inventory. As in the area of aggression, largely consistent results were obtained in the different samples and with somewhat different instruments. This fact should increase the confidence in the conclusions arrived at, as previously pointed out.

A summary analysis of differences between bullies and whipping boys on individual statements of the Q instruments (which contain exactly the same statements) gives the following result: The bullies and the whipping boys were reliably differentiated on 15 of 55 individual statements according to the boys' Q sorts, on 24 statements according to the mothers' Q sorts, and on 34 statements in the Q inventory (two-tailed test and .10 significance level; if a .05 level is used, the corresponding figures were 11, 22, and 29, respectively). In view of the fact that the reliability of individual statements is normally rather low, the number of differentiating statements must be considered surprisingly high, at least as regards the mothers' Q sorts and the Q inventory. The results show that the bullies and the whipping boys were very different in a number of respects. These differences will be elaborated below.

The summary results above also suggest that the boys very likely experienced some difficulties in describing themselves by means of the Q sort technique. First, the mothers of the boys differentiated the bullies and the whipping boys on many more items than did the boys themselves. In addition, the bullies and the whipping boys were separated on even more statements, according to the boys' self-descriptions through the Q inventory. Since the groups of bullies and whipping boys used in the first and the second Solna investigations may be regarded as roughly equivalent, the conclusion may be drawn that the Q-sort technique was less appropriate for boys of this age (around 13) than a conventional inventory format. This, of course, does not say anything about the relative merits of these two formats for somewhat older subjects. The results, however, make it natural to attach relatively more importance to the mothers' Q sorts and to the Q-inventory data in the following analyses.

In the results obtained, the whipping boys stand out as generally more anxious, insecure, and nervous than other boys, both bullies and well-adjusted boys, and boys in general (control boys). The whipping boys were more often beset by feelings of maladjustment and inadequacy. They also showed more anxiety about specific situations such as speaking up in class and being alone at home. In addition, the whipping boys gave a more negative evaluation of themselves and their situation, with the exception of the contact with their parents. The whipping boys tended to feel weaker and more isolated among peers at school.

Considering the results from the area of aggression—both whipping boys and well-adjusted boys were found to be generally nonaggressive, as will be recalled—it is now also of interest to look more closely at the well-adjusted boys. These boys were generally secure, confident, and positive about themselves and their own situation. Taken together, the above results provide strong support for the assumption that the generally non-aggressive behavior of well-adjusted boys and whipping boys originated from different sources or, in other words, it was a manifestation of quite different psychological dynamics.

Thus the nonaggressive behavior of the whipping boys seems to be largely determined by their anxiety and insecurity, by incapability or fear of aggressive reaction patterns: They could not or dared not be aggressive or assertive toward their peers, not even in self-defense in situations characterized by attacks, ridicule, and provocations from other boys.[4]

The nonaggressive behavior of the well-adjusted boys, on the other hand, reflected a fundamentally different situation: They felt secure and confident, they were well liked and seldom attacked or ridiculed by their peers. In addition, there were certain signs suggesting that they very likely could manifest (and probably had manifested) aggressive or assertive behavior when attacked or provoked. As will be recalled, the well-adjusted boys were more prone than the whipping boys to protest against a frustrating teacher, and they felt to a greater extent (Mother's Q sort) that a boy should be able to take a few knocks.

With regard to anxiety and self-confidence, the bullies were better off than boys in general and the whipping boys in particular. They felt more secure, less afraid, and less anxious, and had on the whole a positive attitude toward themselves and their situation, with the exception of the contact with their parents. In the area of anxiety, the bullies appeared in fact to be fairly similar to the well-adjusted boys. One may of course wonder whether the bullies' self-assurance and relative lack of anxiety—as measured by the instruments used—were just a facade, a kind of compensation for insecurity existing under the surface. Perhaps the bullies' answers to one statement in the

---

[4] It was emphasized earlier that the whipping boys, taken as a group, were physically weaker than boys in general. It might be assumed that their high degree of anxiety and insecurity was a simple consequence of physical weakness. That this was not the case, however, is evident from the following: The 7 whipping boys in the first Solna investigation who were judged by the teachers as physically weaker than average were no more anxious or insecure (according to the Q sorts of the boys and their mothers) than the 12 whipping boys who were assessed as average in physical strength (for 2 of the whipping boys, information was lacking on physical strength).

self-evaluation form might be taken as support for this line of
thought: The bullies had a slight, though not significant, tendency to agree to a greater degree than the whipping boys and
the control boys with the statement "I am often afraid of
having nightmares," $p = .31$. This tendency, however, was con-
tradicted by the results on several other statements that can also
be said to concern more indirect signs of anxiety, such as: "I am
often afraid of getting sick," and "I am often afraid that
something unpleasant will happen to me." Moreover, the
teachers' descriptions of the Solna boys, to be reported on in a
later section, support the view that the bullies were fairly sure
of themselves and fearless, possibly with the exception of a
small number of them.

Of course, there may be grounds for assuming that many of
the bullies were characterized by some kind of basic insecurity,
but it should be emphasized that if this assumption is correct,
their lack of security lay so deep that neither the bullies
themselves, their mothers, nor their teachers seemed to notice it.
Thus, if there was a basic insecurity in the bullies, there are
several reasons for assuming that it was essentially different in
character and form of expression from the kind of insecurity
characterizing the majority of the whipping boys.[5]

With regard to contact with the parents, it was primarily the
bullies who differed from the other groups. They seemed to
have a less positive attitude to their fathers and to their parents

[5] Of interest in this connection are the results from a special projective
technique, the Defence Mechanism Test (Kragh, 1960, 1969), used in the
first Stockholm investigation. In this technique, "threat stimuli" are
presented to the subject in a special apparatus (a tachistoscope) with very
short exposure times. Thus this method is completely different from the
methods used until now. One "sign"—no. 2, the one that occurred most
frequently—distinguished among the three groups: The well-adjusted boys
had the lowest values, the bullies came next, and the whipping boys had
the highest values, $F (2, 32) = 5.63, p < .01$. The bullies had somewhat
lower values than the group as a whole ($n = 113$), but they were not
distinguished significantly from the well-adjusted boys. The whipping boys,
however, had significantly higher values than both the bullies and the
well-adjusted boys. On the (common) assumption that the relative occurrence of "sign 2" can be taken as an indication of the subject's degree of
anxiety and "defense" (in the psychoanalytic sense), the well-adjusted boys
were least and the whipping boys most characterized by anxiety and
defense. In any case, the results did not support the assumption that the
bullies were more anxious than boys in general.

generally, they felt less well liked by them, and they had more often wanted to run away from home. In general, the results indicated less strong and less positive bonds between the bullies and their parents. The results for the whipping boys and the well-adjusted boys, on the other hand, pointed to closer contact and more positive relations between the boys and their parents.

The main points of this section, based on reports made by the boys and their mothers, can be summarized as follows.

- The whipping boys were generally more anxious, insecure, and nervous, and they evaluated themselves and their situation more negatively, with the exception of their relations with their parents.
- The bullies were more secure, less afraid, and less anxious and on the whole evaluated themselves and their situation more positively. The results indicated, however, less strong and less positive relations between the bullies and their parents.
- The well-adjusted boys, like the bullies, were more secure and less anxious and evaluated themselves and their situation more positively, including their relations with parents.
- The generally nonaggressive behavior of the whipping boys seemed to be largely determined by their anxiety and insecurity, by incapability or fear of aggressive reaction patterns. The nonaggressive behavior of the well-adjusted boys reflected a fundamentally different situation.

RELATIONS TO SCHOOL

Methods and Results

The boys' relations to school and teachers can be highlighted in several ways from the available data: from the teachers' assessments of the boys' ability to profit from instruction, from the grades, and from the boys' answers to the attitude inventory Our Class.

As mentioned, the main teachers also used the checklist discussed in Chapter 6 for assessing the boys' ability to profit from instruction. Only three grades were employed: poor, average, and good. As might be expected, there was a high correlation between these assessments and the boys' grades received at the end of the spring term, $r = .77$ between teacher assessments and average grade in "theoretical" subjects, $n = 64$.

With regard to ability to profit from instruction, no significant differences were found between the whipping boys, the bullies, and the control boys in the first Solna investigation (Comparison I, p. 81, χ^2 test, $df = 4$, and Fisher's exact probabilities test).

In the second Solna investigation (Comparison II, p. 81), there was a tendency in the direction of significant overall differences between the groups, $\chi^2 (4) = 8.00$, $p = .10$. The whipping boys appeared in the poor category somewhat more frequently than the control boys, $p < .05$ (Fisher's exact probability test), but the differences were not great.

In the first Solna investigation, grades were available for the three special groups ($n = 64$). The statistical analyses (by means of one-way analysis of variance, t tests, and χ^2) were focused on the grades in the theoretical subjects (separately and in combination), which have been found to correlate substantially (around .60) with measures on intelligence tests. The main results were: (1) There were small and nonsignificant differences between the bullies and the whipping boys. (2) The grade-point average for the bullies as well as for the whipping boys was slightly but not significantly below the "expected grade-point average" of 3.00.[6] (3) The grade-point average for the well-adjusted boys was significantly above the "expected grade-point average," $p < .005$, and also above the average grade of the whipping boys and the bullies, $p < .005$.

The results of the first Solna investigation were in all essentials replicated and corroborated in the second Solna study.

[6] Quote from the report book: "A grade of 3 is given when the pupil's achievements are judged to correspond to the average for all the pupils in the country taking the same course." The grade-point average for theoretical subjects was 2.86 for the whipping boys and 2.81 for the bullies. When the whipping boys and bullies who were in some kind of special class (7 boys in all) were excluded from the analyses, the grade-point average for theoretical subjects was 2.83 for the whipping boys and 2.98 for the bullies. For the combination of Swedish and mathematics, the average grades were 2.87 and 3.03, respectively.

There was thus no significant differences in average grades between the whipping boys, the bullies, and the control boys, although the first two groups tended to have slightly lower grades than the control boys.

Data from the Our Class inventory (the first Solna investigation) were used to throw light on the boys' attitude to schoolwork and the teachers. It is primarily scales I, III, and IV (p. 60) that are of interest here. As previously mentioned, data were lacking on 7 of the 21 bullies (and on 1 of the 21 whipping boys and 1 of the 60 control boys). This fact may have slightly affected the average values for the group of bullies, most probably in the direction of giving somewhat more positive values than if all the bullies had answered the inventory. However, the presence of such a bias can to some extent be checked since four of the six statements in scale I were also included in the self-evaluation form. For this form, complete data were obtained from all 11 bullies and 10 whipping boys (and the 60 control boys) in the second Stockholm study. The data in both studies were analyzed by means of one-way analysis of variance.

No significant differences appeared between the groups in either the Solna or the Stockholm studies. This was true for the scale values (composites) as well as for the individual statements. Some trends may be noted, however. In the Solna investigation, the whipping boys had the least negative attitude to schoolwork (scale I), whereas the bullies and the control boys were almost alike. In the Stockholm investigation, the bullies were more negative to schoolwork than the nearly equal whipping boys and control boys, but the difference was not significant here either, $p = .17$. With regard to attitude to teachers (scales III and IV), the whipping boys in the Solna investigation appeared to be somewhat more positive and the bullies somewhat more negative than the control boys, $p = .22$ for scale III and $p = .35$ for scale IV. Thus it was possible to note a tendency toward a more negative attitude to teachers and schoolwork among the bullies and a more positive attitude on the part of the whipping boys. This tendency was weak, however, also in the Stockholm investigation (scale I), where the bully group was complete.

Comments

The results show that both the whipping boys and the bullies were fairly average—or possibly slightly below average—as regards school achievement and "ability to profit from instruction." These findings may be related to different hypotheses that have been put forward in the discussion on mobbing problems: (1) It is the most gifted pupils, or perhaps the pupils who do well in school, who tend to become whipping boys. (2) It is the less gifted or less successful pupils who tend to become whipping boys. The present results do not clearly support either of these hypotheses. And it should be noted that the analyses also tested and rejected the combined hypothesis that the group of whipping boys was composed of *both* particularly gifted *and* less gifted boys (and especially few boys in the middle range).

Of course, it cannot be ruled out that particularly good or particularly poor school results may in individual cases have been one factor (among several) contributing to whipping boy problems. However, on the basis of the results obtained, it may be asserted that factors such as these seem generally to be of little or no importance for the appearance of whipping boy (and bully) problems (see also Chapter 8). For comparison, it can also be pointed out that the well-adjusted boys, whose level of school achievement was generally high, were to only a very small extent exposed to attack and irritation from other boys.

With regard to attitude to schoolwork and the teachers, a slightly more positive tendency was found among the whipping boys and a somewhat more negative one among the bullies. The tendencies were weak, however (not significant).

It may also be mentioned that the general attitude to schoolwork and the teachers appeared to be fairly positive—perhaps surprisingly so, given the age group concerned. The typical answer to statements of the type "I get bored in school" was close to *sometimes* ($n = 247$). And the boys thought that the teachers *often* "explained things very well."

The main points from this section can be summarized as follows.

- Both the whipping boys and the bullies were average—possibly slightly below average—as regards school achievement.

- The results did not support the assumption that the level of the boys' school achievement is an important factor for the appearance of whipping boy problems.
- The whipping boys showed a somewhat more positive and the bullies a slightly more negative attitude to schoolwork and the teachers than a randomly selected control group.

TEACHER ASSESSMENTS OF WHIPPING BOYS AND BULLIES

As previously stated, the teachers gave a free description of the boys picked out as whipping boys, bullies, and well-adjusted boys. In many cases, these appraisals provided very lively pictures of the behavior patterns of the individual boys. It is, however, a well-known fact that such assessments can be unreliable or distorted, for instance, due to particular conflicts between the assessor and the assessed, or through the assessor having particular assumptions about the nature of the problems. It is therefore natural that "soft" data of this kind be employed with some caution. At the same time, it is obvious that the teachers who in many cases had known the boys for several years were in possession of much valuable information that could be related to what has been obtained by other methods. It may also be recalled that the teachers' classification of the boys as whipping boys and bullies proved to be both reliable and valid (see Chapter 4).

Since the teachers were given a fairly free hand in describing the boys, there was naturally considerable variation with regard to the completeness and amount of detail included in the descriptions. The following points, referring to the whipping boys in the first Solna investigation, are worth emphasizing. For a very large part of the boys in this group, the teachers used expressions that, more or less directly, could be interpreted as indicating anxiety and sensitivity. Words such as "anxious, nervous, kind, sensitive, quiet, retiring, fearful, and insecure" were very common. Similar expressions that in addition reflected the whipping boys' passive and nonaggressive behavior when attacked were: "doesn't fight back, doesn't answer back, gives way, withdraws into his shell, cries easily." Seven or eight of the boys were described by the teachers as "overprotected." Further comments showed that the teachers were thinking primarily of parents who were overanxious, who protected their boys in a "wrong" way or wrapped them up in cotton, so to speak. Some of the boys were described as being "too well brought up": "courteous, polite, very tidy, perfect, precocious."

Three of the whipping boys deviated noticeably on some points from the remaining 18. They were hot-tempered and came easily into conflict with other boys (they also had high values on two or three of the aggressive peer-rated dimensions). They were also described as irritating (e.g., "they meddle in affairs that do not concern them"), tension-creating, and restless. Two of these boys had been assessed as fluctuating to some degree between being whipping boy and bully. These boys were obviously somewhat different from the majority of the whipping boys. I will come back to this point in the next chapter.

The previously drawn conclusion that the whipping boys did not have a teasing or provocative manner was also supported by the teacher descriptions. There were two or three exceptions, however, and two of them were whipping boys who had been characterized as hot-tempered.

The teachers described the majority of the bullies with expressions that could be interpreted as indicating a strong need for dominance or aggressive self-assertion: "wants to dominate and assert himself, forces others to obey him, a type who orders others about, enjoys being the boss, shows an enormous capacity to lead in a negative way." Toughness and self-assurance were also stressed: "unusually tough manner, eggs others on in a tough way, a type that must always get his own way, self-assured, insolent, uninhibited, derisive." Many were regarded as irascible and, in my interpretation, as having a low frustration tolerance: "has a violent temper, flares up over nothing, can't bear criticism, can't bear losing, easily angered if things go against him." For several of the boys, it was said that they incited others to violence: "urges others on to physical attack, gets X to use physical force, likes setting others up against Y, carries the others with him." It was also generally pointed out that other boys, who were ordinarily fairly nonaggressive, now and then joined in the activity of attacking and harassing the whipping boy.

For a few of the bullies—perhaps five or six—there were also remarks in the descriptions suggesting "nervous disturbances": "aggressive, nervous and tense, restless, lacks concentration, problem child with great contact difficulties, makes trouble in order to get attention." It must be emphasized, however, that this type of nervous disturbance—perhaps a kind of nervous hyperactivity—which according to the teachers was characteristic of a few of the bullies, was something quite different from the quiet anxiety typical of the majority of the whipping boys.

Generally, the teachers' observations were in agreement with the results obtained by the methods previously described. At the same time, they provided some additional information of value. For example, they gave a good picture of the character and quality of the bully's way of relating to his peers. Furthermore, it became clear that the bullies often incited other boys to harass and attack the whipping boys. The information from the teachers thus confirmed but also supplemented the results previously arrived at. To summarize:

- The teacher descriptions were in agreement with, and on some points supplemented, the previously obtained picture of the whipping boys and the bullies. Many of the bullies were characterized by strong needs to dominate, and they were often described as inciting others to attack. The parents of several of the whipping boys were characterized as overanxious and as parents who "wrapped their boys in cotton."

SOME DATA ON SOCIAL BACKGROUND

In the analyses reported so far, little has been said about the boys' developmental background and home conditions. In the last section, some information about the teachers' view of certain parents was given and the Q sort (Q inventory) provided some data on the boys' contact with their parents. In addition, the present section will report some analyses of the parents' social group membership, their education and age. However, a thorough analysis of factors in Sector D in the theory sketch will not be possible until the parental interviews from the second and third Solna investigations have been examined in detail. Here, only a few preliminary results from these studies will be reported. The following analyses were made by means of χ^2, Fisher's exact probabilities test, and one-way analysis of variance.

Certain social data were available for the three special groups in the first Solna investigation. On the basis of the father's occupation, or the mother's in the father's absence, a division into three social groups was made, in accordance with the social groupings of the official election statistics (see, e.g., Boalt & Husén, 1967). No significant differences in social group membership were found between the parents of the whipping boys, the well-adjusted boys, and the bullies ($n = 64$). Very similar results were obtained for an index combining the social groups established separately for the mothers and the fathers. Nor were there significant differences between the groups with regard to the amount of the father's or the mother's education.

Analysis of the socioeconomic data from the second and third Solna investigations gave results that were in agreement with what was reported above. In these studies, a number of more refined indexes were also constructed, combining the parents' amount of education, annual income, standard of housing, and so on. No significant differences were found among the parents of the whipping boys, the bullies, and randomly selected control boys, neither for the simple nor the refined indexes of socioeconomic status ($n = 91$ in Solna II, $n = 65$ in Solna III). Obviously, the socioeconomic status of the parents (the boys) seems to be of no importance for the appearance of whipping boy/bully problems.

The fathers of the whipping boys were on the average somewhat older than the fathers of the bullies and the well-adjusted boys in the first Solna investigation, $F = 2.96, p = .06$. Also, the whipping boys' mothers were slightly older than the mothers in the other groups, but the differences were not significant. These trends, however, were not confirmed in the second and third Solna investigations.

In summary:

- No differences in socioeconomic status were found between the parents of the whipping boys, the bullies, the well-adjusted boys, and randomly selected control boys. The socioeconomic status of the parents (the boys) seems to be of no importance for the appearance of whipping boy/bully problems.

SOME STABILITY DATA

In Chapter 5, data were presented that showed a considerable degree of stability over a 1-year period in whipping boy/bully characteristics as perceived by teachers and also in the peer-rated dimensions Start Fights and Aggression Target. In that context, it was anticipated that a more comprehensive stability study involving more classes, raters, and variables over a longer period of time would be presented in this chapter. It is obviously of great interest to get information on the stability of dimensions or characteristics clearly related to whipping boy/ bully problems—factors in Sector C of the theory sketch. The results of such stability studies, particularly if there has been a certain amount of identifiable environmental change during the interval, may have important implications for the conceptualization of the problems discussed. I will now present a follow-up study covering a 3-year interval. Since the details of the study have been reported elsewhere (Olweus, 1977a), only a summary description will be given here.

Method

The subjects were 201 boys from 18 classes in the first Solna investigation who were rated by classmates at the end of grade 6 and also 3 years later, at the end of grade 9, when their median age was 16 years. In grade 6, the 18 classes contained a total of 214 boys. In the follow-up, 13 of these boys had disappeared from the present schools, and 27 new boys had entered the classes. The new boys constituted roughly 12% of the boys in the present classes in grade 9. Two classes to be commented on later had undergone marked changes in the composition of the peer group. Furthermore, all classes had new teachers in grade 9, and 11 of the classes had moved to other school buildings. A certain amount of environmental change had thus occurred from grade 6 to grade 9 for this subject group.

The variables rated were Start Fights, Verbal Protest, Aggression Target, and Unpopularity (see p. 24; the scoring of the last variable was reversed in the present study). The number of raters in the different classes varied somewhat, the average being four in grade 6 and five in grade 9. In general, the raters were randomly selected from each class. Approximately a third of the raters on the second occasion had also served as raters in grade 6. No evidence was found that use of some of the same raters on both occasions led to inflated stability correlations and, accordingly, it was considered justified to regard the two rater groups as independent.

In order to make the ratings from different classes more comparable, the average ratings were converted within each class to standard scores (z scores). By this procedure, differences in mean level and variability between classes and grades were eliminated.

The reliabilities for average ratings of four raters (grade 6) were estimated to be .83 (Start Fights), .86 (Verbal Protest), .73 (Aggression Target), and .81 (Unpopularity). The corresponding values for average ratings of five raters (grade 9) were .86, .88, .77, and .84.

As is well known, a stability correlation between two sets of measurements on a particular variable is systematically lowered (attenuated) as the result of errors of measurement. Accordingly, the correlation between true or error-free scores on the same variable would be higher than between fallible scores. By means of the formula for the correction for attenuation (e.g., Lord & Novick, 1968), it is possible to compute the disattenuated correlation, that is, an estimate of the correlation between corresponding true or perfectly reliable scores. If, as in the present context, the primary interest lies in assessing the relationship between the true rather than the obtained scores, that is, the stability of the "underlying" function(s) in contrast with the actual predictive power of the falliable measurements, a disattenuated coefficient is the most appropriate measure to use (Block, 1963, 1973; Thouless, 1939). In consequence, attenuation-corrected stability coefficients will be reported in addition to the uncorrected "raw" correlations. The coefficients used are product-moment correlations.

TABLE 14

Uncorrected and Attenuation-Corrected Stability Correlations
for a 3-Year Interval ($n = 201$)

Variable	Uncorrected correlation	Corrected correlation
Start fights	.65	.77
Verbal protest	.70	.81
Aggression target	.56	.75
Unpopularity	.71	.86

Note. The coefficients reported are product-moment correlations; r values of .14 and .18 are significant at the .05 and .01 levels, respectively.

Results and Comments

The main results are presented in Table 14. The stability correlations were high and, especially with regard to the attenuation-corrected coefficients, of similar magnitude for all four variables. The results imply that only small changes in the boys' relative positions had occurred during the 3-year period. Those boys who were highly aggressive or nonaggressive, respectively, in grade 6 tended to behave in a similar way 3 years later. And those who were unpopular or the target of other boys' aggression, respectively, in grade 6 were in large measure the least liked or the most attacked boys in grade 9.[7] There was thus a high degree of stability in the functions measured for the period covered.

In addition, in the report on the 3-year follow-up (Olweus, 1977a), a study on 85 boys from another population was presented. The boys in this sample were followed for a 1-year interval, from grade 6 to grade 7, and the same four rating dimensions were used. As expected, the stability correlations were even higher in this study, the attenuation-corrected coefficients ranging from .87 to 1.00.

[7] Although there was a significant decrease from grade 6 to grade 9 in the mean level for Start Fights and Aggression Target, and a significant increase for Verbal Protest, the differences were fairly small ($r_{pb} < .20$, $n = 201$). These analyses were carried out on the untransformed data.

TABLE 15

Average Intercorrelations across Grade 6 and Grade 9
for the Four Rating Variables ($n = 201$)

Variable	2	3	4
1. Start fights	.69	.03	.13
2. Verbal protest		.08	−.11
3. Aggression target			.53
4. Unpopularity			

Note. The coefficients reported are product-moment correlations; r values of .14 and .18 are significant at the .05 and .01 levels, respectively.

Before accepting these results, however, it is necessary to evaluate in detail the data and methods upon which the correlations are based. Among other things, it is important to consider to what extent the ratings reflected factual characteristics of the ratees as opposed to cognitive structures or biases in the raters (see, e.g., Mischel, 1968; Wiggins, 1973). In the detailed report of the study (Olweus, in 1977a), several analyses of this and similar points were undertaken, and it was generally concluded that the results consistently and convincingly attested to the validity and general adequacy of the ratings employed in the present study.

The pattern of intercorrelations between the four rating variables were very similar in grade 6 and grade 9. The average intercorrelations across the two grades are presented in Table 15. It will be seen immediately that the fairly common pattern of relationships in rating studies—with substantial, positive correlations among all or most of the variables rated—was not found in the present investigation. On the contrary, there were several correlations of zero order. In particular, it is worth emphasizing that the two aggressive variables correlated about zero with the popularity variable. This fact strongly suggests that the ratings were not made in terms of some overall evaluative dimension, for instance, on the basis of generalized halo tendencies in the raters. Furthermore, the approximately zero correlation between the aggressive variables and Aggression Target shows that the raters could make a clear distinction regarding the direction of aggressive responses: There was no connection between the extent of being the target of other boys' attacks and a boy's own aggressive behavior. As expected, the two aggressive variables correlated substantially with each other, and there was also a relatively high correlation between the variables Aggression Target and Unpopularity. The results reported are in agreement with what has been found previously for the same variables in similar subject groups (e.g., Olweus, 1973a, p. 309).

In evaluating the stability results obtained (Table 14), it should be recalled that a certain amount of environmental change had occurred during the 3-year interval under study. As pointed out, all teachers in grade 9 were different from those in grade 6. And change of school did not seem to appreciably affect the degree of stability over time. There were small and inconsistent differences between the across-time correlations for the 11 classes that had moved to other school buildings and the 7 classes that had not moved.

In addition, a certain amount of exchange of classmates had taken place. In this context, two classes are of particular interest. In one of these, the original sixth-grade class consisting of 10 boys was split into two at the beginning of the eighth grade, 5 boys being transferred to another class (for unknown reasons). At the second period of rating, the original class had been augmented by 8 new boys (with no previous connections with each other), which thus represented a very marked change in the composition of the class. This notwithstanding, the stability correlations for the 5 original boys were very high, in fact even higher than the corresponding correlations for the total sample ($n = 201$). Also, the transfer of the 5 boys to a new class consisting of 9 boys did not seem to reduce the stability in behavior of the 9 boys. The across-time correlations for the core of 9 boys were without exception higher than the coefficients for the total sample. Although the number of subjects involved was small, these results suggest a high degree of stability in the dimensions under study in spite of considerable changes in the composition of the peer group.

Furthermore, it may be generally assumed that there was at least a certain amount of pressure from the teachers and the school administrative staff in the direction of modifying the behavior of the highly aggressive pupils. As evidenced by the high stability correlations for the aggressive variables, such environmental pressure did not seem to be very effective. It may also be taken for granted that at least a certain proportion of the boys who were unpopular and/or the target of other boys' aggression actively tried to bring about changes in the relationships with their peers. Apparently, such attempts were largely unsuccessful.

All in all, these results show that only small changes occurred over a 3-year period in dimensions or characteristics clearly related to whipping boy/bully problems, in spite of a good deal of environmental variation and the existence of certain forces presumably acting to effect changes in these respects. Among other things, this implies that the highly aggressive boys did not in general "outgrow" their aggressive reaction patterns. Furthermore, it means that a certain fraction of the boys (at least 5% according to the estimates presented earlier) were exposed to hard and humiliating treatment from their peers over long periods of time. And the majority of the boys who were unpopular in grade 6 continued to have low peer status over the 3-year interval studied. At least for a certain portion of the unpopular individuals, this is likely to represent a very difficult situation that may have considerable effects on their immediate as well as later adjustment. Combined with the previously reported results, these findings have other important implications, which will be discussed in the interpretive summary to be presented in the next chapter.

It should be noted that the findings reported in this section are in agreement with, corroborate, and extend the general conclusions about the character of the whipping boy/bully problems drawn in Chapter 5 (p. 74).

The main results of this section can be summarized as follows.

- In a 3-year follow-up, a high degree of stability over time was found in the dimensions studied, which are clearly related to whipping boy/bully problems. The highly aggressive boys did not in general "outgrow" their aggressive reaction patterns. And those boys who were unpopular and the target of other boys' aggression, respectively, in grade 6 were in large measure the least liked and the most attacked boys in grade 9. These results were obtained in spite of a good deal of environmental variation and the existence of certain forces presumably acting to bring about changes in these respects.

8

AN OVERALL PICTURE OF WHIPPING BOY/ BULLY PROBLEMS

INTERPRETIVE SUMMARY

In the preceding chapters, a great many empirical findings have been reported. Although a number of conclusions and interpretive statements have also been made, it is now essential to present a condensed and integrated view of the factors that seem to be of greatest importance for the appearance and development of the problems under consideration. The reader who wants to get an overview of the empirical results may read through the summaries presented at the end of each chapter in Chapters 4-6 and at the end of each section in Chapter 7. An account of samples and methods is given in Chapter 3.

First, it may be recalled that a considerable number of "structural" or "system" variables such as the size of the school and the class, the teacher's satisfaction with her or his work, the teacher's way of conducting the schoolwork, and the group climate of the class were included in the research design (variables from Sector A). It was considered important to find out whether structural factors such as these were associated, possibly causally, with the degree of whipping boy and/or bully problems in a class. Although the research design provided ample opportunity to prove that structural factors were relevant to the problems under study, such was not the result.[1]

The Bullies

In view of these findings, it was a natural next step to direct the attention to what has been called organismic or person factors, that is, factors characterizing individual boys (Sectors B and C). In particular, if the boys selected as bullies or whipping boys were distinguished by special characteristics, this might provide valuable information about factors of relevance for the appearance and maintenance of the problems under consideration. In these respects, a number of significant and marked differences between bullies, whipping boys, well-adjusted boys, and control boys were obtained. As expected, the bullies were much more aggressive, both physically and verbally, against peers as well as teachers, than the boys in the other groups. They were also characterized by a positive attitude to violence and violent means. There was thus a considerable degree of consistency in aggressive reactions across different situations.

Furthermore, and most important, the aggressive behavior was found to be quite stable over time, over a 1-year as well as a 3-year interval.[2] Although it might be tempting to construe this behavioral consistency as evidence for a corresponding consistency of some reaction tendencies or motive systems "within" the boys, this cannot be done without further analyses. The observed consistency over time might, for instance, be primarily a reflection of stable differences in environmental conditions for different individuals. Accordingly, the conclusion about the high degree of stability over time may in the first

[1] Of course, the influence of structural factors may be studied in different ways, and it is possible that additional analyses might have revealed some significant relationships. The total pattern of results, however, suggests that structural factors are likely to have weak effects (if any) on these problems.

[2] The stability studies were not restricted to the behavior of the bullies. Although there is not a one-to-one relationship between teacher-named bullies and boys rated as very aggressive by their peers, the bullies had very high values on the aggressive rating dimensions. They also constituted a very large portion of the highly aggressive boys.

place be said to apply under "typical conditions," that is, under a degree of environmental variation and pressure for change typically found in the lives of the subjects for the periods studied. What this may mean in more detail has to be found out by additional analyses.

It may then be recalled that a certain amount of environmental change had taken place between the first period and the later periods of investigation. The high degree of stability in aggressive behavior was obtained in spite of changes in teachers, school buildings, size of the school, and classmates. Furthermore, it may be generally assumed that there was at least a certain amount of pressure from the teachers and the administrative staff in the direction of modifying the behavior of the highly aggressive boys. As evidenced by the high stability correlations, such pressure did not seem to be effective. It may thus be concluded that the behavior of the highly aggressive boys was to a large extent maintained irrespective of a good deal of environmental variation and in opposition to social forces presumably acting to change this same behavior. The high degree of stability becomes even more remarkable in view of the possibility of variations due to developmental changes during the 3-year period studied.

It is natural to ask, however, whether there were not particular aversive situations or conditions in the school environment of the bullies that might "explain" their behavior. It should be noted that the bullies were not attacked or teased by their peers more often than boys in general. Consequently, their aggressive behavior cannot be interpreted as some kind of defensive reaction in response to frequent attacks or provocations from other boys. In addition, the bullies enjoyed almost average popularity among the boys (and possibly more than average popularity among the girls). Accordingly, the highly aggressive behavior cannot be explained as a result of peer rejection.

With regard to school achievements, the bullies were average or slightly below average. Their aggressive behavior was not particularly directed against the successful pupils, as might have been expected, if they saw themselves as failures in the school system. The possible effects of the school system will be dealt with in more detail in a later section (p. 163), but the conclusion may be anticipated here. On the basis of several lines of evidence, it will be concluded that the highly aggressive behavior of the bullies can hardly be explained as a consequence of frustrations and failures in the school setting.

The previously reported results on the psychological picture of the bullies are in agreement with such a conclusion. Among other things, it was found that the bullies, according to self-reports as well as reports from their mothers, felt nonanxious, confident, tough, and had on the whole a positive attitude toward themselves. They were also physically stronger than boys in general. Furthermore, the bullies did not come from lower socioeconomic levels than the other groups and, accordingly, their aggressive behavior cannot be accounted for as some sort of compensatory reaction in response to feelings of social inferiority in the school setting. Finally, it should be pointed out that attacking and bullying other children may a priori be considered to reflect mainly self-initiated activity, a kind of activity over which the individual may be assumed to exercise a substantial degree of "control" (see Olweus, 1977a).

In sum, it is very difficult to explain the behavior of the highly aggressive bullies as a consequence of their being exposed to unusually aversive situations or conditions in the school setting. All these findings and considerations converge on the conclusion that very important determinants of the observed consistency in aggressive behavior and reactions, across different situations as well as over time, are to be found in relatively stable, individual-differentiating reaction tendencies or motive systems within the boys (see Olweus, 1976). This conclusion stresses the view that to a considerable degree the highly aggressive bullies actively select and create the kind of situations in which they are often observed (see Bowers, 1973; Wachtel, 1973). In other words, the bullies may be said to be characterized by an *aggressive personality pattern*, with a tendency to react aggressively in many different situations, with fairly weak controls or inhibitions against aggressive tendencies, and with a positive attitude to violence.

No detailed analysis of this personality pattern and its motivational dynamics will be attempted in the present context.

It may be mentioned, however, that this pattern, in terms of my conceptual framework presented elsewhere (Olweus, 1969, 1973a), seems to correspond to a combination of high habitual aggressive tendencies and predominantly low habitual aggression inhibitory tendencies. On the basis of the results obtained, it is natural to assume that the attacking and harassment of weaker boys give rise to feelings of superiority in the bullies and also provides them with a certain prestige, at least among some of their peers (chiefly instrumental aggression, see, e.g., Olweus, 1973a). In addition, it is probable that hurting and humiliating the victim are in themselves satisfying to the bullies (chiefly hostile aggression). A discussion of some of the factors likely to be responsible for the development of a highly aggressive personality pattern will follow in a later section of this chapter.

The fact that personality factors are heavily stressed in the interpretation of the aggressive behavior of the bullies should not be taken to imply that their behavior is unaffected by situational factors. In my view, knowledge of the strength of an individual's habitual aggressive tendencies cannot in general lead to very accurate predictions of the behavior of that individual in a particular, concrete situation. In order to make more precise predictions for particular situations, it seems necessary to take several additional factors into account (see Olweus, 1969, 1973a).

The Whipping Boys

In the group comparisons, it was generally found that the whipping boys were more anxious, insecure, unpopular, and had lower self-esteem and a more negative attitude toward themselves than boys in the other groups. They were also physically weaker. In addition, the peer ratings showed that they were generally nonaggressive. These general findings notwithstanding, the teacher descriptions of the individual boys make it natural to distinguish between two different types of whipping boys. The overwhelming majority of the whipping boys were characterized in the ways described above, and they will be named *passive whipping boys.* A small number, however, were found to be of another kind, more actively irritating, tension-creating, and restless. They were also considered to be hot-tempered and, when attacked, they reacted differently from the passive whipping boys: They got angry and fought back, or at least attempted to fight back. A closer look at the peer ratings also revealed that they had obtained high values on two or all three of the aggressive dimensions, in addition to having been rated as unpopular and the frequent target of other boys' aggression. As regards anxiousness, self-esteem, and other areas studied, there seemed to be small and inconsistent differences between the passive whipping boys and these boys. The latter type of whipping boy will be called the *provocative whipping boy*. In the first Solna investigation (grade 6), only 3 out of 21 whipping boys belonged to the provocative category. Similar results were obtained for the second Solna investigation (grade 6), 4 out of 19 being characterized as provocative whipping boys. In all probability, somewhat different mechanisms are operative in classes with provocative whipping boys. In consequence, it is valuable to maintain the distinction between passive and provocative whipping boys in some of the following sections, but main emphasis will be placed on situations involving whipping boys of the predominant, passive category.[3]

In the 3-year follow-up, a high degree of stability was found in the two dimensions on which the whipping boys had high values, Aggression Target and Unpopularity. Also, this stability was obtained in spite of a certain amount of environmental change (with respect to teachers, schools, classmates) and, presumably, certain efforts on the part of at least some of the whipping boys to bring about changes in their peer relationships. In this connection, it is natural to ask whether the whipping boys themselves actively contributed to their being the target of other boys' aggression, for instance, by way of a teasing behavior. With the exception of the small number of provocative whipping boys, this was clearly not the case, as previously pointed out: The passive whipping boys had very low values on the peer-rated dimensions Tease, Start Fights, and Verbal Protest

[3] In this connection, one may ask whether there were also different types of bullies. This question deserves further attention, but in the present investigation there is no basis for such distinctions. It is more reasonable to regard the earlier-suggested variations in a few points (p. 123) as differences of nuance.

(even when the provocative whipping boys were included, the mean values for the whipping boy group were lower than those for the control boys, see Table 3, p. 44). And in the total group ($n = 201$), there was essentially no connection between the extent of being the target of other boys' attacks and a boy's own aggressive behavior (see Table 15, p. 128). Thus the considerable amount of aggression directed against the passive whipping boys cannot be explained as a consequence of their being themselves aggressive or actively provocative. This conclusion is corroborated by the previously cited findings regarding the psychological and physical characteristics of the whipping boys—their general anxiousness, lack of self-esteem and toughness, often combined with physical weakness. On the basis of these results and rational considerations of the nature of the Aggression Target variable (see also Olweus, 1977a), it is reasonable to conclude that the passive whipping boys were often in situations not desired by themselves but forced upon them. To a large extent, they were simply the victims of violent attacks, teasing, and oppression from other boys, in particular the highly aggressive bullies. For the same reasons, the Aggression Target variable may be interpreted as primarily reflecting an aspect of each boy's interpersonal environment.

The high across-time correlations for the Aggression Target dimension thus shows that this aspect of the environment was consistently different for different boys. There is no indication, however, that this individual-differentiating environmental stability can account for the high stability correlations for the aggressive dimensions, as previously discussed. On the contrary, it is more reasonable to assume that the environmental constancy reflected in the Aggression Target variable was in considerable measure a consequence of the high stability in the aggressive dimensions.

As mentioned, the stability was also high for the Unpopularity variable. Even if low peer status reflects a number of different things (see, e.g., Hartup, 1970), it is obviously impossible to explain the unpopularity of the passive whipping boys as a consequence of their being aggressive and actively provocative (see above). As with the Aggression Target dimension, it is reasonable to conclude that the high stability correlation for Unpopularity indicated consistently different environmental conditions for different boys. For at least a large portion of the whipping boys, it may be assumed that their low peer status was not something desired by themselves but rather forced upon them.

However, the high degree of stability in this dimension, even in the two classes in which great changes in the composition of the peer group took place, clearly suggests that the whipping boys possessed certain characteristics that tended to make them unpopular in a variety of groups and situations. Included among such presumably important aspects are the attributes previously described. Without developmental data, however, it is difficult to know for sure to what extent the psychological characteristics of the whipping boys (in grade 6) were a consequence rather than a cause of their being rejected and attacked by other boys. More certain information on these points will emerge when the parent interview data have been analyzed. On the basis of rational considerations and the information currently available, it can be generally assumed that characteristics such as those suggested—a certain sensitivity and anxiousness, lack of assertiveness and self-esteem (often in combination with relative physical weakness)—were present at a fairly early age in these boys and directly contributed to their being rejected by their peers. At the same time, the peer rejection is likely to have increased the (potential) whipping boys' anxiousness and lack of self-esteem and, consequently, it is natural to regard these characteristics as, to some degree, an effect as well as a cause of their being disliked by peers.

A boy with characteristics such as those described is thus likely to be unpopular in many situations and groups. Such a boy may be regarded as vulnerable, but it is reasonable to assume that he will not become the target of open attacks and oppression from other boys, an actual whipping boy,[4] unless he enters a group with one or several highly aggressive boys—(potential) bullies. This means that accidental

---

[4] As previously stated, a distinction is made between actual and potential whipping boys (and bullies). The term "actual whipping boy or bully" is used only when the problems have been present for somewhat longer periods of time.

circumstances—if the peer group includes or does not include (potential) bullies—will very likely play a role in determining whether an unpopular, potential whipping boy will develop into an actual whipping boy.

The above results and considerations lead to the conclusion that personality and, to some degree, physical characteristics (weakness-strength) of individual boys—potential whipping boys and bullies—must be assigned great weight in explaining the appearance and maintenance of the problems under consideration. The implications of this conclusion will be elaborated upon in later sections of this chapter. The conclusion, however, does not imply that social psychological factors are of negligible importance for whipping boy and/or bully problems. Several mechanisms of a social psychological nature are likely to be involved, as will be discussed in a later section.

MAIN TYPES OF SITUATIONS

On the basis of the interpretive summary, a more detailed picture of the problems under consideration will now be drawn. It is desirable to distinguish four main types of situations represented in different classes in the Solna investigations. These types of situations correspond to the categories implied by the formulation "whipping boy and/or bully problems" in the theory sketch.

In the classes studied, the following situation was by far the most frequently found: problems involving one passive whipping boy (or several) and one bully (or several). In some classes of each grade, there were whipping boys, but no particular boy was judged to be a bully. In addition, there were a few classes with bullies but no particular whipping boys. These three situations are naturally designated, respectively, as classes with whipping boy and bully problems, classes with whipping boy problems, and classes with bully problems. As mentioned earlier, there were also a few classes in each grade that, according to the teacher, were entirely without problems of this sort.

I will start by drawing a picture of the most common situation, involving whipping boy and bully problems. Afterward, the other main types of situations will be discussed more briefly. The following account is primarily based on results from the sixth-grade samples, when the boys were roughly 13 years old, but it is very likely that the same or similar mechanisms are operative at lower and, to some degree, at higher age levels.

Whipping Boy and Bully Problems

A Concrete Picture

Among the boys in a class, there are normally some conflicts and tensions of different kinds. Usually there are also many slight aggressive interactions, partly for fun, as a form of self-assertion and for the testing out of strength relations among the boys. If there is a potential bully (or several) in such a group, this will influence the boys' activities. The interactions will be rougher, more vehement and violent. The irascible temperatment of the bully,[5] his marked needs to assert himself, to dominate and subdue others, make themselves strongly felt. Even minor adversities and frustrations lead to intense reactions, which often assume an aggressive form because of his inclination to use violent means in conflicts. Due to the physical strength of the bully, his aggressive attacks are often unpleasant and painful to others. Even if he prefers to attack the weakest boys, whom he is certain of defeating, he is also not afraid of starting fights with other boys in the class. Generally, he feels rather tough and self-confident.

If there is also a potential passive whipping boy in the class—anxious, insecure, fearful of being assertive and aggressive, and often physically weak as well—he will soon be discovered by the bully. He is the weak link in the chain, the one who does not retaliate when he is attacked, who becomes afraid and perhaps cries, who is unwilling or unable to ward off attacks by even fairly harmless antagonists. Generally, he disapproves of taking part in rough games with the other boys of the class. He also feels rather alone and isolated.

For a boy with bullying tendencies, the potential whipping boy is an ideal target. His anxiousness, defenselessness, and crying give the bully a marked feeling of superiority and supremacy, also a sort of satisfaction of vague revengeful impulses.

But the bully usually wants to have others join him, and he soon induces his closest friends to pick on the whipping boy. There is always something in the looks, clothing, or manners of the whipping boy that can be attacked. Often, it is equally pleasant for the bully to

---

[5] For convenience, the terms "bully" and "whipping boy" are often used in this section instead of the more correct designations "the potential bully" and "the potential whipping boy," respectively.

see other boys harass the whipping boy as to do it himself. And after all, he keeps a line of retreat open, if there should be unpleasant consequences. But the adults at school frequently do not pay attention to the fuss, or they are not in the vicinity and let the boys themselves settle their conflicts. The whipping boy does not seem to say much to his parents.

Now and then other boys in the class are also active in harassing and teasing the whipping boy. He is a safe target for attack: Everybody knows that he is weak and does not dare to retaliate, and none of the stronger boys in the class stand up for him. When some of the tough boys in the class have attacked him, it can hardly be a fault to harass him a little. After all, he is rather miserable and valueless, he almost deserves a beating.

Gradually, the whipping boy becomes more and more isolated among the peers. His already low status in the peer group is further impaired by the open teasing and attacks: It is obvious to everyone that he is good for nothing. It appears that some of the boys are afraid of reducing their own status or of incurring contempt or disapproval by being together with the whipping boy. Some may even be afraid of ending up in the same situation. At last, the isolation has become almost complete.

The picture presents a number of essential elements of a situation in which whipping boy and bully problems develop. Since it represents a *schematized account*, it cannot of course incorporate individual variations and particular circumstances. An attempt has been made, however, to give a relatively concrete picture of the development of such problems in a class, by mingling different perspectives: how the situation is likely to be or to appear for a bully, a whipping boy, and other boys; some factual, descriptive data of importance have also been included.

Mechanisms

Several of the mechanisms involved in the preceding account could be related to different psychological concepts and research results. It is beyond the scope of this book, however, to undertake a more complete linkage of the results examined here to other psychological research. I will just suggest some principles of more general importance. In this section, the focus will be on mechanisms that are likely to operate in the peer group and the school situation. Later on, I will deal with some conditions contributing to the development of the personality pattern characterizing the (potential) bully and the (potential) whipping boy.

As mentioned earlier, the bully often has a few relatively close friends who are under his influence—who perhaps have the same tendencies as himself, though less pronounced. It is not difficult for the bully to set these boys against the whipping boy.

But why do other, more "neutral" boys now and then harass the whipping boy, as was evident from the teacher descriptions? The following mechanisms are likely to be particularly relevant: (1) social "contagion," (2) weakening of the control or inhibitions against aggressive tendencies, (3) distribution of responsibility, and (4) cognitive changes.

With regard to the first mechanism, several studies have shown that both children and adults tend to imitate the behavior of another person (a "model") who is acting aggressively (see, e.g., Bandura, 1973; Berkowitz, 1965). The imitative effect is stronger if the observer is frustrated and if the model's aggressive behavior seems justified. As an explanation of this phenomenon, it has been assumed that the stimulation provided by the sight of another person's aggressive behavior tends to activate similar reaction tendencies in the observers (or at least in some of them). Furthermore, the sight of an aggressive model (the bully) easily conquering a weak opponent (the whipping boy) can arouse positive expectations in some boys/observers, that is, expectations of a successful outcome in an aggressive interaction with the same opponent. This can stimulate the observer's desire to assert himself and to raise himself in the other boys', and perhaps also in his own, estimation. However, it is clear that not all observers (boys) react in the same way to viewing a model. Those who are most influenced by this kind of model can be assumed to be somewhat uncertain boys, who do not have a high status among their peers, and who would like to increase their prestige (see, e.g., Shaw, 1971). They may not like the bully, but they are likely to admire his fearless behavior, his toughness, and his physical strength. Such *aggression-stimulating effects* can be described with partly synonymous concepts such as social facilitation (Allport, 1924; Berkowitz,

1962), modeling influence with vicarious reinforcement (Bandura, 1973), and social contagion (Redl & Wineman, 1957). The concept of contagion has also been used to describe similar phenomena among apes in captivity (Russel & Russel, 1968).

The other central mechanism was referred to as a weakening of the control or inhibitions against aggressive tendencies. This concept is also related to a body of psychological research. It has been found out that when an observer sees a model rewarded for aggressive behavior, there is a tendency for the observer's own inhibitions to be reduced. On the other hand, if the aggressive behavior leads to negative consequences for the model, inhibitory processes are often activated or strengthened in the observer, at least temporarily (Bandura, 1973; Berkowitz, 1962). In a whipping boy/bully situation, this may operate in several different ways. First, the bully is directly rewarded by his victory (this is also related to the first mechanism). The bully escapes uncomfortable and painful consequences, since the whipping boy usually does not fight back. And there is little risk that the other boys will attack him in defense of the whipping boy, since the whipping boy has little support in the class. Moreover, the bully seems to run little risk of incurring punishment from the teachers or from other adults. On the basis of the available data, it is difficult to be definite about the teachers' attitudes and behavior with respect to whipping boy/ bully problems. Certainly, there are rather large differences from teacher to teacher in this matter. It seems very probable, however, that many teachers do not "see" what the boys are doing, possibly because they believe it is best for the boys to work things out among themselves. If the teacher is in the vicinity and does not intervene, this is naturally interpreted as adult approval of the bully's (and others') aggressive behavior. Results consistent with such an explanation have been obtained in several experimental studies (e.g., Berkowitz, 1962). It is also possible that the bully and his friends practice some of their activities secretely, so as to avoid possible interference from the teachers. Furthermore, the whipping boy apparently talks as little as possible to his parents about his school situation, perhaps due to fear of retaliation from the bully. In consequence, the bully has little reason to be afraid that the whipping boy's parents will take up the case with either the teacher or the principal. Besides, it is probable that the bully is skilled at talking his way out of the trouble (according to teacher descriptions). Thus it can be concluded that under typical existing conditions, the bully's behavior is not likely to incur negative consequences from either the whipping boys, the classmates, the teachers, or the parents of the whipping boys. Moreover, the bully's behavior brings about a reward in the form of victories (as well as the satisfaction of internal hostile tendencies and self-assertion needs). All of these may contribute to a reduction of aggression controls in a number of boys/ observers. There is reason to assume that this effect is most marked in boys who have rather strong aggressive as well as aggression-inhibitory tendencies (Olweus, 1969).

As previously suggested, the bully and his "henchman" play a central role in creating and maintaining this type of problem in a class. But the two mechanisms mentioned can contribute to an explanation of why other boys—who are ordinarily "nice, though perhaps somewhat inconsiderate and too easily influenced"—also go on the attack against the whipping boy from time to time.

In addition to these mechanisms, the effects of a distribution of responsibility should be mentioned in cases where several boys join in the harassment. It is well known from social psychology, that an individual's feeling of personal responsibility for a negative activity tends to decrease to the extent that other individuals take part in it (see, e.g., O'Neal & MacDonald, 1976). Moreover, cognitive changes occur as a consequence of the repeated open attacks on the whipping boy: Eventually the whipping boy is perceived as rather worthless and almost deserving of a beating. These two mechanisms may help reduce possible guilt feelings in the occasional, or quasi, bullies. As for the real bullies, with low inhibitions and a generally positive attitude toward violence, there is little reason to believe that they have any marked guilt feelings about their behavior.

It is important to emphasize that far from all of the boys in a class take part in the harassment of the whipping boys. It appears, for example, that the well-adjusted boys contribute to a very small degree or not at all. Why are these boys not susceptible to the mechanisms mentioned above? Several factors can explain this: (1) These boys are relatively secure, confident, independent, well liked by their peers, and they probably find little satisfaction in defeating the whipping boy (it satisfies self-assertion needs only to a small degree). (2) They have rather weak (habitual) aggressive tendencies, which implies that they find little satisfaction in inflicting injury or discomfort on the whipping boy, unless they have been provoked. (3) They have strong (though not excessive) controls over aggressive tendencies, and they have a negative attitude toward violence. In other words, they have an internal system of norms that would probably lead to self-criticism and guilt feelings if they went along with attacking a rather defenseless whipping boy. On the basis of these points, it may be inferred that the well-adjusted boys are somewhat critical of the bully (at least passively); the bully clearly does not function as a model for them.

Classes with Whipping Boy Problems

Having discussed the most common situation, I shall now briefly touch upon what was earlier designated as whipping boy problems. The most striking aspect about the few classes of a grade that had marked whipping boy problems but no special bullies seems to be that the whipping boys were of a different kind: They were not of the passive type discussed in the previous section, but they belonged to the provocative category. As mentioned the provocative whipping boys were described as hot-tempered and generally irritating, and they were often unruly and distractible. Even though they were assessed primarily as whipping boys, some of them were described as being able, in some degree, to change between the whipping boy and bully roles. This duality was also reflected in the peer ratings.

This description indicates that the mechanisms involved had a different character from those discussed previously. The whipping boys' behavior in the classes appeared to be actively tension-arousing and provocative, and it had the effect of releasing aggressive reactions from a rather large number of pupils. Occasionally, the whole class would turn against them. It is probable, however, that the absence of particular bullies was merely due to the circumstance that no boys with marked bully tendencies were found in these classes. In the first Solna investigation, one of the three provocative whipping boys was a student in a class that also had a bully. This shows that such a combination can also occur.

Classes with Bully Problems

In some classes, there were bullies but no particular whipping boys. The girls in the class might occasionally become the bully's target, or sometimes pupils in other classes would be attacked. Periodically, several of the boys in the class were exposed to the bully's aggressions, but not in such a way that anyone, according to the teacher, could really be called a whipping boy. There may exist several different explanations for the absence of whipping boy(/bully) problems here. On the basis of the results examined earlier, it seems most likely that in these classes there were no clear potential whipping boys. But it is also conceivable that some of the boys in the class had ganged up on the bully and to a certain degree put him out of action. The analyses conducted so far do not permit definite conclusions on this point.

Classes without Problems

Several possible interpretations also exist for the few classes that, according to the teachers, had no problems of this nature. This will be evident in the following overview.

WHEN ARE WHIPPING BOY AND/OR BULLY PROBLEMS LIKELY TO APPEAR IN A CLASS?

The previous analyses will now be summarized in a schematic account of the factors that seem to be of greatest importance for the appearance of whipping boy and/or bully problems. Here the emphasis is on an assessment of the likelihood that such problems will appear in a class. The most likely outcome of some combinations of factors will be suggested. In accordance with the previous analyses, personality and physical factors characterizing individual children—as reflected in the concepts of potential whipping boys and bullies—are assumed to play a central role. In addition, a new concept, situational pressure, is introduced. It should be noted that the following presentation is not built upon strict empirical tests of different combinations of factors. Rather, it represents probability judgments on my part, based primarily on the empirical results obtained, but also on general theoretical considerations. I will take up only a few main points. The social psychological mechanisms likely to be operative in a class with problems of this kind (p. 143) will not be discussed in the present context.

The following account is based on what seems to be the typical existing situation: There are no strong group norms against peer violence in the class, and the teachers interfere only to a limited or unimportant degree. To the extent that harassment of individual children is met with "counter forces" in the form of definite group norms and active intervention from teachers, this is likely to affect the situation considerably. I will come back to this point in the next chapter.

It seems important to maintain the earlier distinction between the two different types of whipping boys, the passive and the provocative. This distinction will be the basis for the presentation to follow.

Situations in Which a Potential Passive Whipping Boy is Present/Absent

The presence or absence of a potential bully in the class seems to be crucial for the appearance of problems in this type of situation. If the group contains a potential bully and, in addition, a potential whipping boy of the passive type, there are strong reasons to expect that whipping boy and bully problems, as previously described, will arise in the class. But if the group contains a potential bully, but no potential whipping boy, only a bully problem is likely to appear. This implies that the bully's aggression is not so markedly directed against one particular boy, but affects some or many of the boys in the class. This type of problem can be said to be less serious, in that no single student becomes the object of intense, continuous harassment. But if a new potential whipping boy comes into such a class, the result will probably be a whipping boy/bully problem.

This argument is based on the idea that the potential bully is, so to speak, "activated." By this I mean that there is *situational pressure*, that is, particular conflicts and tension-producing conditions that affect the bully's personality (dispositions) and activate his need for aggressive self-assertion and domination. This implies that the potential bully's personality problems can be "dormant" due to weak situational pressures. It is also possible that his special motivational dynamics may have become channeled into relatively constructive paths. If the potential bully in a class is not activated, one can speak of either a *latent (or neutralized) whipping boy/bully problem or a latent bully problem.* It is probable, however, that the problems will become manifest if situational pressures on the potential bully increase or if the prevailing balance is disturbed.

The broad and somewhat vague concept of situational pressure has been introduced in order to generally signify different types of conflicts and tension-creating conditions that can activate the potential bully's personality problems. Although little empirical knowledge of situational pressure is currently available, it is reasonable to presuppose the presence or absence of such pressures in consideration of the fact that, according to the teachers, there may be relatively marked variations over time in the intensity of bully/whipping boy problems in a class. Furthermore, a bully's change of class may sometimes result in a clear reduction of his aggressive behavior. It is natural to assume that the source of situational pressure may be found in the school setting, in the home, and in leisure settings.

Next to be considered are the situations in which the class lacks a potential bully, and either has or does not have a potential whipping boy. On the basis of the results obtained, it can be assumed that the passive whipping boy does not create much tension or irritation in the class. As a rule, he is anxious, unobtrusive, and he prefers to be by himself—at least, if it is impossible to have friends in the group. A potential whipping boy of this type must of course take his knocks in coexisting with the other boys, but if the class does not have a special bully, a whipping boy problem would not be likely to occur. The most fortunate classes from this point of view are those that have neither a potential whipping boy nor a potential bully.

In sum, the argument above implies that the presence or absence of a potential whipping boy in a class is of secondary importance for the appearance of mobbing problems. But if the class contains a potential bully, the nature of the problems will be affected: The absence of a potential whipping boy will probably result in the development of bully problems, whereas the presence of a potential whipping boy is likely to lead to the development of whipping boy/bully problems.

Situations in Which a Potential Provocative Whipping Boy Is Present

In contrast to what applies to the passive whipping boy, tension and irritation arise easily around the potential provocative whipping boy. If a potential bully is also in the class, it is probable that the provocative whipping boy's behavior will activate the bully (if he has not already been activated by other causes) and a whipping boy/bully problem will arise. But even if there is no potential bully, a whipping boy problem can be expected. Since the provocative whipping boy irritates many students in the class, the probability of more collective reactions increases. This fact can contribute to the appearance of a possible whipping boy(/bully) problem that contains unusually strong collective elements. This reasoning can be summarized thus: The presence of a potential provocative whipping boy in the class is probably a central factor in the development of whipping boy, or whipping boy/bully problems in these situations. The problems seem to have a somewhat different character; among other things, there are more collective elements than in the situations discussed in the preceding section.

As with the potential bullies, there is reason to expect that the presence or absence of situational pressure will regulate the activation of the provocate whipping boy's personality problems. If the situational pressure is slight, or if the whipping boy's motivational dynamics have settled into a kind of equilibrium, one can speak of a latent problem in the class.

At present, the personality problems of this kind of whipping boy are less clear than those of the passive whipping boy and the bully. This is related to the fact that provocative whipping boys were much less common than passive whipping boys, as previously mentioned.

WHAT PREDISPOSES AN INDIVIDUAL BOY TO BECOME A BULLY?

This question can be understood in several ways. In this section, I will suggest some answers to possible interpretations.

If one looks at the problem from a limited perspective, it is evident that several of the analyses presented in this book constitute an answer, in any case for the age groups and conditions studied. Earlier in this chapter, there is a description of several characteristics of typical bullies. In particular, the bullies were found to be characterized by what was called an aggressive personality pattern: strong aggressive tendencies, weak aggression inhibitions, and a generally positive attitude toward violence. It is obvious that a boy with such characteristics is more likely than other boys to become a bully (he may not be an actual bully in his class). If a boy of this type comes into a new class, he must be regarded as a potential bully, and the probability of whipping boy/bully problems in the class is likely to increase.

If, however, the problem raised in the question heading this section is to be answered more thoroughly, two important additional questions present themselves (1) To what extent is the presence of an aggressive reaction pattern in a boy stable over time? (2) Are there genetic factors or particular conditions in the immediate environment or in the developmental history of highly aggressive boys that can explain their behavior and attitudes?

Longitudinal Aggression Studies

With regard to the first question, data have already been presented in this book that showed a high degree of stability in aggressive dimensions over a period of 3 years, from grades 6 to

9. In addition, the verbal descriptions in connection with the teacher assessments in grade 6 indicated that many boys had been bullies for several years. Nevertheless, a broader perspective on this issue may be gained from a brief overview of the results from some other longitudinal aggression studies.

A recent review (Olweus, 1976) of 15 longitudinal studies of aggression (mainly American studies), containing a total of 24 stability coefficients (including 2 coefficients reported in this book, Chapter 7), shows, first, that the stability correlations presented in this book are in general agreement with the results obtained in other studies. The studies reviewed were quite varied, including widely different methods and covering time intervals from 6 months to 21 years. The age of the subjects at the time of first measurement varied from approximately 2 to 18 years. The average number of subjects on which a stability correlation was based was 116. The review was limited to studies in which male subjects were used (4 studies on mixed nursery school groups were also included).

Furthermore, when the stability correlations (corrected for attenuation, see Lord & Novick, 1968) were plotted as a function of the interval in years between the two times of measurement (T_2-T_1), a relatively regular picture was obtained (see Figure 4). As might be expected, the size of the stability coefficient tends to decrease as the interval covered increases.[6]

Since behaviors associated with intelligence and cognitive processes have been generally regarded as possessing a high degree of stability over time, it is of interest to compare the results from the aggressive area with data from the intelligence domain. Figure 4 also shows the regression line for stability data on intelligence test measurements compiled by Thorndike (1933). In this case, the regression line was based on 36 stability coefficients (corrected for attenuation) covering intervals up to 5 years.[7] These coefficients were derived from 13 different samples of school-age children; the average sample size was 111.

[6] The trend can be described by the following regression equation $Y = .78 - .018X$ where Y is the disattenuated correlation and X the interval ($T_2 - T_2$) in years.
[7] The regression equation describing the trend in Thorndike's data is: $Y = .92 - .022X$.

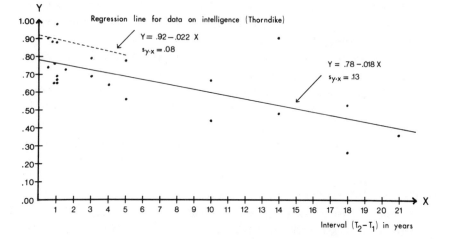

FIGURE 4. Regression line showing relationship between attenuation-corrected stability coefficients (product-moment correlations) in the area of aggression and interval in years between times of measurement. The regression line is based on 24 stability coefficients (plotted). For comparison, the regression line for attenuation-corrected stability coefficients in the area of intelligence (Thorndike, 1933) is shown (broken line). This regression line is based on 36 stability coefficients (not plotted).

As is evident from the figure and the regression lines, the stability of the intelligence measures was slightly higher than for the aggressive variables (but the decrease of the regression line was somewhat steeper than for aggression). On the basis of these results, it may be generally concluded that there is a substantial degree of stability over time in aggressive reaction patterns[8] (as well as in intelligence). The difference in stability in the two areas does not appear to be great.

For purposes of illustration, three of the longitudinal studies constituting the basis for the above conclusion will be briefly described.[9] In an early study (Jersild & Markey, 1935), 24

---

[8] The term "aggressive reaction *pattern*" is used to indicate that very often an aggressive variable studied refers to several subclasses of behavior or reactions or that two or more intercorrelated aggressive variables, e.g., verbal and physical aggression, have been studied.

[9] More detailed descriptions are given in Olweus (1976).

nursery school children aged 2 to 4 years were observed at two points in time, separated by approximately 9 months. The behavior of each child was recorded during 10 distributed 15-minute periods of free play. Marked individual differences in aggressive behavior were found, and the behavioral stability was striking. When calculated for all 24 children, the stability correlation over the 9-month period was .70 (rho) for the variable or primary interest, "Frequency of being aggressor." When the correlations were determined separately for different groups (n varying from 7 to 15), the coefficients were even higher (range .71– .88). After correction for imperfect reliability, the stability correlation of .70 increases to .88. This means that from the first to the second period of observation, very small changes had occurred among the children in their tendency to attack other children: Those children who were frequently aggressive toward their peers at the beginning of the study tended to behave in the same way 9 months later, and so on. It should be noted that this high degree of stability in aggressive behavior was obtained in spite of the fact that relatively marked changes in the composition of the peer groups had taken place from the first to the second time of observation. The results of the Jersild and Markey study are in agreement with those obtained by Patterson, Littman, and Bricker (1967), which were mentioned briefly in Chapter 2.

In another study, Eron, Huesmann, Lefkowitz, and Walder (1972) collected longitudinal data at three different periods of time, when the subjects were in grade 3 (8 years old), in grade 8 (13 years old), and when they were approximately 19 years old, for convenience designated as grade 13. The basic measure of aggression was a peer-nomination instrument in which each subject could be nominated by other subjects for a number of items describing aggressive behavior (e.g., "Who starts a fight over nothing?" "Who says mean things?"). The essential validity of this peer-nomination measure has been demonstrated in several studies, including teacher ratings (Walder, Abelson, Eron, Banta, & Laulicht, 1961) and controlled experimental situations (Williams, Meyerson, Eron, & Semler, 1967).

The stability correlation for the period from grade 3 to grade 8 (n = 71) was .48, after attenuation correction .56. For the period from grade 8 to grade 13 ($n = 71$), the corresponding coefficients were .65 and .78 (corrected). For the longest interval, the approximately 10-year period from age 8 to 18–19 ($n = 211$), the uncorrected stability correlation was .38, and the corrected one was .44. It may be mentioned that similar results were obtained for the female subject groups. It was also found that the eighth-grade aggression measure predicted later antisocial behavior with considerable success.

The final study to be described briefly was carried out by Jack Block (1971) and presented in *Lives Through Time*. The subjects of this study were 84 adolescent males (and 87 females), participants in the well-known Oakland Growth and Berkeley Guidance longitudinal studies. By means of the Q-sort method, the subjects were assessed for three different periods of time, the junior high school years (JHS), the senior high school years (SHS), and when they were in their middle thirties (Adult). For each subject, three independent sets of data, one for each period, were developed, and this material was used to characterize each subject on a number of variables. The characterizations of the subjects were made by clinical psychologists who worked independently and who were assigned to "cases" in systematically permuted combinations, in order to avoid judge biases. At least two of the variables included are directly concerned with aggressive reactions and behavior: "Overreactive to minor frustrations; irritable" (no. 34) and "Tends to be rebellious and nonconforming" (no. 62).

The stability correlations for the first of these variables, "Overreactive, etc.," were .45 for the JHS–SHS period (an interval of 3 years) and .29 for the SHS–Adult period (an interval of approximately 18 years). After correction for attenuation, these coefficients were .78 and .40, respectively. For the variable "Tends to be rebellious, etc.," the stability correlations for the JHS–SHS and the SHS–Adult periods were .58 and .29, after attenuation correction .72 and .37, respectively. When a composite was formed of these two variables, the disattenuated stability correlations were .69 for the JHS–SHS period and .53 for the SHS–Adult period (see Olweus, 1976).

In evaluating these results, it should be noted that a good deal of environmental change had occured in the lives of the subjects during the 20 or so years from the high school years to the time of the adult follow-up. Among other things, 95% of the subjects had married, and 19% had been divorced. The majority of them had become parents. Roughly half of the subjects had also served in the armed forces during World War II.

As mentioned, the review in which the three studies were included shows that there was generally a substantial degree of stability in aggression over time, often over many years. In addition, it should be emphasized that marked individual differences in habitual aggression level were found to manifest themselves early in life, certainly by the age of 3. It is also worth noting that the results from the various studies formed quite a regular and consistent pattern in spite of the fact that there was great variation among the studies in sample composition, definition of variables, research setting, method of data collection, and the researcher's theoretical orientation.

As pointed out in the interpretive summary at the opening of this chapter, however, a high degree of stability over time in a particular area cannot without further analyses be taken as evidence for a corresponding stability of some reaction tendencies or motive system "within" the boys. In particular, it is important to get some knowledge of the degree of environmental change characterizing the lives of the subjects during the periods under study.

When the studies were examined for actual and presumed environmental changes and pressures for changes during the periods studied, the degree of stability manifested was even more surprising. On this point, the review (Olweus, 1976) concluded: "In an overall appraisal, . . . the primary task confronting the researcher becomes one of explaining the substantial stability or lack of change in aggressive behavior found to prevail in spite of considerable environmental variation and in opposition to a number of influences acting to change this same behavior (p. 60)" The related conclusion was also drawn that there appears to be little evidence supporting a view that stable diferences in aggression level result from consistently different environmental conditions for different individuals in the situation in which the aggressive behavior is displayed—in the nursery school, the school, etc. (However, the conditions in other situations, e.g., the family, may have been and may still be at the time of the study quite different for aggressive and nonaggressive individuals; see the next section.)

On the basis of the review of these studies including the longitudinal results presented in this book, the following three general conclusions may be drawn: (1) There is a substantial degree of stability in aggressive reaction patterns, often over many years. In response to the question discussed in this section, it may thus be concluded that, in general, the presence of an aggressive reaction pattern in a boy is not a transitory phenomenon; such patterns are likely to show a considerable degree of stability over time, especially if the boy has reached the age of 8-9 years or more. (2) It is difficult to explain the behavior of highly aggressive boys as a consequence of particularly aversive or provoking conditions in the situations in which the aggressive behavior is typically displayed (in the school, in the nursery school, etc.). (3) All in all, the pattern of findings leads to the conclusion that very important determinants of the observed stability in aggression over time are to be found in relatively stable, individual-differentiating aggressive tendencies or motive systems in the boys (see, e.g., Olweus, 1969, 1973a). Note that a highly similar conclusion was reached in the interpretive summary at the beginning of this chapter, but in the present context the basis of the conclusion has been considerly broadened.

The Development of
Aggressive Reaction Patterns in Boys

The above conclusions naturally lead to the second of the two questions previously posed: Are there genetic factors or particular conditions in the immediate environment or in the developmental history of highly aggressive boys that can explain their behavior and attitudes? Part of this question has already been answered on the basis of the longitudinal studies: As was stated in conclusion 2, it is difficult to explain the behavior of the highly aggressive boys as a consequence of particularly aversive or provoking conditions in the situations in which the aggressive behavior is typically displayed.

What, then, about genetic factors? It must be immediately admitted that, at present, very little is known about the potential influence of genetic factors as a basis for individual differences in habitual aggression levels in humans (among boys). In animal studies, the effects of selective breeding on aggressive behavior have been demonstrated in a large number of species (e.g., Becker, 1962; Scott, 1958). In the area of human aggression, however, very little research has been directed to the issue of possible genetic effects (see Cattell, Blewett, & Beloff, 1955; Heise, 1973; Jinks & Fulker, 1970). Although relevant human data are thus largely missing, it seems reasonable to assume that genetic factors play some, but probably a small, role in determining individual differences in aggressive behavior among boys. It is also possible that certain other personality characteristics such as degree of extraversion, which seems to have a relatively strong genetic component (e.g., Eaves & Eysenck, 1975), may interact with particular kinds of socialization practices (environmental conditions) and in this less direct way be of some importance for the development of aggressive reaction patterns. In sum, although more definite conclusions cannot be drawn due to a paucity of research findings, it may be tentatively assumed that individual differences in aggression level among boys are only to a rather small extent (if at all) determined by genetic factors (see Heise, 1973).

It is now appropriate to direct attention to a number of child-rearing studies that have attempted to isolate factors of importance for the development of highly aggressive reaction patterns, particularly in boys. Only an overview of the main findings will be presented (for more detailed descriptions and references, see Becker, 1964; Berkowitz, 1962; Eron, Walder, & Lefkowitz, 1971; Feshbach, 1970).

In a large number of studies, two broad dimensions of parental attitudes/behavior (affective relations) have been found. They may be described as (1) a hostility versus warmth dimension: To what extent are the parents, respectively, hostile/rejecting or warm/accepting in their basic attitude? and (2) a permissiveness versus restrictiveness dimension: To what extent are the parents, respectively, permissive (possibly lax) or restrictive. The second dimension generally concerns the extent to which parents place demands and restrictions on their children.

These two dimensions have also been found to be important in the development of aggressive reaction patterns. A number of studies have shown that highly aggressive boys often have parents (mothers have been studied most frequently) who have been hostile, rejecting, negative, or indifferent in their basic attitude. In addition, the parents have not, as a rule, placed consistent demands on the boy for reasonably controlled and nonaggressive behavior (the parents have been highly permissive or lax). Thus the parents of very aggressive boys have often been characterized by a combination of hostility *and* laxness.

Furthermore, it has been found that parents who often use physical punishment and similar "power-assertive" child-rearing methods frequently have aggressive sons. Since it has been shown that the use of punitive disciplinary techniques tends to be associated with a hostile, rejecting attitude toward the child, it is difficult to know whether the obtained relationship is chiefly the result of physical punishment, of parental hostility, or of a combination of punishment and hostility.

In some studies, poor emotional relationships with the father have been emphasized as an important factor. Bandura and Walters (1959), for example, found indications of early disturbances in the father-son relationships of 26 very aggressive middle-class boys, compared to 26 control boys. As teenagers (around 15–17 years), the aggressive boys expressed much more hostility against their fathers, and they were more weakly identified with them. This study also found the earlier-mentioned association between strong aggressive reaction patterns in the boys and a negative, rejecting attitude in the parents.

By and large, the childhoods and family relationships of very aggressive boys stand out as fairly similar in the various studies. Depending on their theoretical orientation, however, researchers have emphasized slightly different aspects in interpreting the findings. At least three mechanisms are likely to be involved. They may function in isolation or, more probably, in combination. (1) A fundamentally negative, rejecting attitude from the parents (possibly associated with physical punishment) is a severe frustration for the boy and creates strong aggressive tendencies and hostility. (2) A hostile and aggressive parent (like other parents) may function as a model for his son. Implicitly, the boy understands the fathers's/mother's behavior as sanctioning and perhaps also as encouraging aggressive behavior on his own part—at least, if it is directed toward other people. (3) In addition, it would seem that a generally lax, undemanding, or inconsistent upbringing markedly impedes the building up of internal aggression-controlling mechanisms, particularly if the emotional relationships between the parents and the boy are poor. In such a case, the boy is not very motivated to internalize possible parental demands.

In this context, is should be pointed out that these analyses are based largely on the assumption that the parent is more powerful and influential than the child in forming the parent-child relationship. Although this is a very plausible assumption, the effects of the child on the parent's behavior and attitudes should not be overlooked, as has been stressed by Bell (1968, 1971), for example. However, little precise knowledge of such effects is currently available in the area of human aggression. It is hoped that analyses of the child-rearing data collected within the present project will shed light on this issue.

On the basis of the available research evidence, it seems reasonable to conclude that the nature of the early (and later) parent-child relationships, as described above, plays a central role in the development of highly aggressive reaction patterns in boys. It would seem that this conclusion is largely valid regardless of the socioeconomic status of the parents (e.g., McCord, McCord, & Howard, 1961).

In addition, it appears that an aggressive boy is in many situations rewarded for his aggressiveness, in the form of prestige, as well as with more concrete benefits (e.g., Bandura, 1973). The study by Patterson et al. (1967) showed, for example, that not less than 80% of aggressive acts in nursery school led to favorable consequences for the aggressive child. The reactions of peers can thus be assumed to strengthen (or possibly to reduce, or modify in other ways) an aggressive reaction pattern in a boy. Furthermore, peers also function as models, whose behavior may, in varying degrees, be imitated (e.g., Mussen, Conger, & Kagan, 1969, pp. 397–403).

In the research project described in this book, the data on the childhoods and early peer relationships of the bullies have not yet been analyzed. However, it is not unreasonable to assume that the bullies in this study are characterized by a developmental history that, by and large, corresponds with what has been outlined above. It is also striking that the results of the Q data relating to identification and closeness to parents (p. 111) fit so well with the pattern suggested here. It should be recalled that the bullies thought they were less well liked by their parents in comparison with what other boys thought, and that they generally had a worse relationship with them. It was also evident that the bullies had a more negative attitude toward and probably also a weaker identification with their fathers. And there is no reason to doubt that they had gotten benefits from their aggressive behavior in many situations.

It is easy to see that a developmental history of the kind suggested might explain, at least in part, a bully's low frustration tolerance and strong aggressive tendencies, his general hostility against the environment, and his positive attitude toward violence. With regard to the bully's self-confidence and relative lack of anxiety, these characteristics might be related to his ability to assert himself and to win prestige among his peers by means of aggressive behavior.

On the basis of the research literature, it is thus reasonable to assume that childhood factors of the type discussed predispose a boy to develop an aggressive personality pattern[10]

[10] In the light of recent American research on the effects of televised violence, it might seem natural to include exposure to television violence as an additional factor of importance for the development of an aggressive personality pattern. However, it should be noted in this regard that according to program surveys, the amount of violence portrayed on Swedish television is but a small fraction of what is usually shown on American television (Comstock & Rubinstein, 1971). Furthermore, in the second Stockholm investigation ($n = 142$), no systematic relationships were found between level of interpersonal aggression and a number of questions about television habits, preference for violent programs, etc. In consequence, it seems most reasonable to assume, at the present stage of knowledge, that televised violence in Sweden has relatively little effect (if any) on the development of an aggressive personality pattern.

and, in a considerable proportion of cases, to become a bully. More precise answers to questions about the strength and character of these relationships, however, will have to await further research.

THE ROLE OF THE SCHOOL
AND THE SCHOOL SYSTEM

Although situational factors have already been discussed several times in the text and have generally been found to be of minor importance for the development of mobbing problems, it is of interest to discuss in more detail a few questions pertaining to the role of the school from this point of view. Can whipping boy/bully problems be seen as a, consequence of the present school system, with its competition and grade pressures? And in particular, can bullying behavior be explained as a response to frustrations and failures in school?

Several answers, both direct and indirect, to these questions have already been given, but an overall appraisal seems in order. I will briefly refer only to those points that have been discussed in earlier sections.

Among the findings obtained, two can be cited that might to some degree support the hypothesis that the bullies' behavior was the result of, or in some way related to, dissatisfaction in school: (1) The bullies tended to have a more negative attitude to schoolwork and the teachers than a group of randomly selected control boys (see Chapter 7). (2) According to the peer ratings, bullies protested much more frequently than other boys when a teacher criticized them for one thing or another (Verbal Protest; see Chapter 4). It should be noted, however, that the tendency in point 1 was weak (not statistically significant). If dissatisfaction and failure in school were of great importance, much more pronounced differences would have been expected on this point, particularly since there were so many marked differences in other areas. As for the result in point 2, it can be related only indirectly to dissatisfaction in school. For now, I will simply emphasize that the bullies' aggressive reactions were in no way directed solely against the teachers: Differences of the same order were also present in the aggressive peer-rated variable Start Fights (with other boys) and Tease (other boys).

In addition, many of the results are difficult to reconcile with the above-mentioned hypothesis, or they even point in the opposite direction. The most important points to consider are:

1. The bullies' grades and their ability to benefit from instruction are average, or possibly somewhat below average (Chapter 7). The bullies can thus scarcely be characterized as "losers in the system." Nor was their aggression especially directed against the most gifted or successful boys, as might have been expected if they felt themseves to be failures; the whipping boys' grades and ability to benefit from instruction were roughly the same as those of the bullies. It should be emphasized, however, that the bullies did not feel unsuccessful; on the contrary, they had a generally positive view of themselves. (That the bullies had a positive view of themselves was also confirmed by their mothers.)

2. No differences in social group membership were found between the bullies, the whipping boys, the well-adjusted boys, and randomly selected control boys (Chapter 7). Thus the bullies' behavior cannot be understood as the result of some kind of social inferiority complex (possibly activated in the school setting) and dissatisfaction associated with it.

3. No systematic positive relationships could be detected between measures of the boys' attitudes to teachers/schoolwork and the incidence of whipping boy/bully problems in the class. Furthermore, there was a striking stability in the peer relationships from grade 6 to grade 7 and grade 6 to grade 9, in spite of the fact that nearly all the classes had new teachers in the later grades. These results would hardly have been expected if dissatisfaction and conflicts with the teacher or a negative attitude to schoolwork were important causal factors (Chapter 5).

4. It is not easy to understand how the bullies' positive attitude toward violence—which is likely to be an essential component in bully problems—could arise as a reaction to dissatisfaction in school.

5. Clear parallels to whipping boy/bully problems have been found in studies of 2–4-year-old children (Jersild & Markey, 1935; Patterson et al, 1967)—long before school and grade pressures begin. As suggested earlier, it is probable that the

foundation for the problems under consideration is laid several years before the child starts school.

6. An assumption that the bullies' developmental history is of the kind suggested in the previous section makes it possible to integrate their reactions and behavior into a meaningful and coherent pattern.

In consideration of these points, the bullies' somewhat negative attitude to school and their strong verbal opposition to a slightly critical teacher must be interpreted primarily as a manifestation of low frustration tolerance and a hostile attitude toward the environment, "authorities" included. These reactions may be regarded as components of a generally aggressive style of life.

The results and considerations suggested above not only fail to support the hypothesis that bullying behavior is a consequence of dissatisfaction and failures at school; all in all, this hypothesis must be considered untenable. The same can be said of the related assumption that whipping boy/bully problems are the result of competition and grade pressures in the present school system (see Chapter 7). Moreover, as has been shown, there are alternative explanations of the factors involved that seem reasonable as well as consistent with the results of this and other studies.

In this connection, it is also worth calling attention to the fact that children, after all, pass only a limited part of their time at school, particularly in the early grades. It should not be necessary to emphasize that prior to beginning school, children have been in day care centers and nursery schools, with peers and siblings inside and out of home and, to a greater or lesser extent, with their parents. In many cases, the problems exist at a relatively early age but may not be clearly recognized until the child begins school.

I will round off this section by making a few brief, general comments on the role of situational factors. The strong emphasis on personality factors and the small weight ascribed to situational factors in explaining the development of whipping boy/bully problems should not be taken to imply that I generally consider situational factors of little or no importance for the explanation and prediction of aggressive phenomena. If, for instance, aggressive behavior in a particular, circumscribed situation is to be predicted, it is, in my view, usually not sufficient to base the prediction on knowledge of the individuals' level of (habitual) aggressive (and aggression-inhibitory) tendencies. In order to make more adequate predictions, situational factors, of an aggressive as well as an aggression-inhibitory character, also should be taken into consideration (see Olweus, 1969, 1973a). Furthermore, the personality problems of a bully may be activated or "dormant," as previously discussed. From this more limited perspective, situational factors in the form of a presumed situational pressure are considered important for whipping boy/bully problems. Finally, it is essential to emphasize that a view stressing personality factors in no way implies an indifference to how the social milieu of the school is shaped. This should be clear from the earlier discussion (pp. 143-147) of the social psychological mechanisms involved in the maintenance of whipping boy/bully problems. This will also become evident in the next chapter, in which questions of what can be done to reduce or eliminate these problems will be dealt with.

WHAT PREDISPOSES AN INDIVIDUAL BOY TO BECOME A WHIPPING BOY?

This question can be interpreted in several ways. I will suggest some answers, but the presentation will be brief since, among other reasons, there seems to be hardly any professional literature that deals directly with the whipping boy phenomenon. I will limit the discussion to the passive whipping boy.

It is obvious that a boy with a pattern of characteristics (or tendencies) such as those found for actual passive whipping boys must be regarded as a potential whipping boy. A certain anxiousness and passivity, fear of being aggressive, and inability to assert himself with peers seem to be essential elements in this pattern, often in combination with relative physical weakness.

With regard to the persistence of whipping boy "behavior," it may be recalled that within the present project, the Aggression Target variable showed a high degree of stability over the 3-year period studied. And the nursery school studies carried out by Jersild and Markey (1935) and by Patterson et al. (1967) found a rather high degree of stability in similar variables, concerning the tendency to be the object of attacks from other children. These children were only about 3 years old, and the time interval covered approximately 8 months. Although few in number, these studies suggest that a boy's tendency to be the target of other children's aggression appears at an early age and may be stable or fairly stable over at least relatively limited periods of time. It should be observed, however, as pointed out in previous analyses, that the tendency to be the victim of other children's attacks is also dependent on accidental factors: the extent to which the peer group includes aggressive children (potential bullies).

Although a whipping boy cannot be defined (only) as a boy with low peer status, is of interest to note that the (un)-popularity variable showed a high degree of stability over the 3-year period covered in the present project. Stability co-efficients generally consistent with these results have been reported in other studies including different age groups and time intervals (see Hartup, 1970).

Little is known about the stability of the personality pattern characterizing (potential) whipping boys. It is not unreasonable to assume, however, that such a pattern is fairly stable and results in the boy's having difficulties in being accepted or liked by his peers, even if he is not actively harassed. In this context, some results from the longitudinal study by Kagan and Moss (1962, Chapter 6) may be cited. In this study, boys who were relatively passive in childhood tended as adults (age 20–29 years) to be socially anxious, to avoid competition with other men, and to be afraid of contact with women. It was also found that boys who were anxious and inhibited in their peer relation-ships at a relatively early age tended to be insecure and anxious in adult social contacts. Even though these results must be interpreted with some caution (for certain methodological reasons), it is not unlikely that passive whipping boys as defined in the present book will tend to develop into adults of the kind suggested by the Kagan and Moss results. In this connection, it may be recalled that the whipping boys were also unpopular among the girls.

Since almost no research literature exists about parent-child relationships and other possibly important aspects of the whipping boys' developmental background, questions about predisposing factors from this point of view cannot yet be answered satisfactorily. Provisionally, it may be suggested that (potential) whipping boys have been somewhat sensitive and passive boys, who have had close contact with their parents, and who have been brought up in an aggression-inhibiting and not very "masculine" atmosphere. The whipping boys' dispositions and the character of their early parental relationships have made them insecure and vulnerable in a peer group. Aversive reactions and attacks from peers have augmented their anxiousness and contributed to giving them a negative self-image, further increasing the psychological distance from their peers.

9

WHAT CAN BE DONE?

Before presenting proposals for solving whipping boy/bully problems, I will summarize some of the main points in the preceding analyses. It is clear that there are serious whipping boy/bully problems in our schools that may continue relatively unchanged for long periods of time. This uncomfortable fact can not be explained away by saying that it really only applies to a small number of boys, or that it is primarily a problem in special classes. Approximately 5% of the boys could be judged to be pronounced bullies, and approximately the same number could be identified as pronounced whipping boys—10% in all. Nor can it be claimed that the problems are limited to schools and classes of a certain size. They are not restricted to boys of a particular social class, nor to those with special external deviations. Without a doubt, these widespread problems must be taken quite seriously.

SOME GENERAL CONSIDERATIONS

What can be done about the situation? Before presenting any proposals, some kind of goal must be stated. Which changes and goals are desirable? It seems appropriate to distinguish between goals for immediate action and goals for more long-term prevention. The research results presented in this book give only an indirect basis for long-term preventive efforts, and I shall therefore deal with this approach to the problem quite briefly. Two general goals for immediate action will be stated. I imagine, perhaps naïvely, that a fairly broad agreement may exist on these goals. Differences of opinion may grow larger when choosing the measures or means for achieving the goals. However, there is some empirical research and general experience to rely on in making these decisions.

Later, I will discuss more fully the problem of who can, or should, take responsibility for the different tasks in such a program of action. Here, I will just emphasize that concentrated efforts by many different groups of people—such as school authorities and personnel, parents, pupils, experts—will be necessary for a satisfactory resolution. As I stressed in the previous chapter, it does not seem reasonable or fair to make the school and the school system responsible for the origin of whipping boy/bully problems. However, this does not rule out the view that it is a natural and essential part of a schools's care for its students to try to limit or prevent these problems.

Of course, it can always be generally asserted that the complex of problems is related to the existing social structure as a whole, and that an analysis must be based on a very broad and comprehensive perspective. Even if one can sympathize in principle with such a point of view, a claim of this kind is hardly appropriate in this context, at least not when it comes to the more immediate measures. This opinion is further supported by the results presented earlier on the effects of the school system and socioeconomic factors. On the basis of the results at hand, I think it is both possible and meaningful to attack the problems from a more limited perspective.

As for the question of measures, I have not considered it appropriate to present detailed proposals, instead, I will restrict myself to a few general guiding principles. These main principles may serve as a basis for more concrete proposals. I also want to point out that it is necessary to have an experimental attitude toward the measures, at least on certain points; various techniques must be tried out and their effects studied. It is certainly advantageous to carry out intervention studies designed as a research project, but informal evaluation in the form of discussions with teachers, students, and parents will also be of great value. In any case, I believe it is very desirable to carry out a program of action, even if there are no possibilities for research evalution. This, of course, does not imply that all courses of action will be beneficial or without harmful effects. It thus seems inevitable that a certain amount of professional expertise must be utilized in planning and following up programs of change. In this connection, I will also note that there is a fairly extensive literature in the social sciences dealing with how to effect change (e.g., Allen, Chinsky, Larcen, Lochman, & Selinger, 1976; Bennis, Benne, & Chin, 1976; Clark, Evans, & Hamerlynck, 1972; Cowen, 1973; Patterson, 1971).

A few general considerations may be added. The following account applies primarily to boys. This is natural since whipping boy/bully problems may be assumed to be much more common among boys than among girls. This assumption is supported by the general experience of teachers and psychologists, and by a number of empirical studies of different reaction patterns and symptoms in boys and girls, respectively (Feshbach, 1970; Maccoby & Jacklin. 1974; Robins, 1966). This notwithstanding, one can assume that whipping boy/bully problems also exist among girls, perhaps in more subtle and indirect forms. Some of the considerations and measures to be discussed in the following sections can probably be applied directly to problems among girls; others, however, must be adjusted to the individual conditions. Furthermore, it is obvious that the measures suggested must be designed differently for students of different age levels.

In the following, I will occasionally use the phrase "repeated physical and mental maltreatment" instead of mobbing or whipping boy/bully problems, because this gives a more concrete idea of what is involved.

GOALS FOR IMMEDIATE MEASURES

The two general goals for immediate action can be formulated as follows: (1) to strongly limit or entirely prevent the occurrence of repeated physical and mental maltreatment in (and preferably also out of) the school setting; (2) to achieve better peer relations in school, and especially to create conditions that make it possible for (potential) whipping boys and bullies to get along and function better in and out of the school setting.

Both of these goals refer primarily to the school milieu, which is a natural point of departure for specific measures. This does not imply, however, that the free-time milieu is unimportant. As will be evident in later sections, I consider it very important that this aspect be taken into account, too.

There is really not much to say about the first goal: I regard it as an absolute requirement that children and young people not be the object of physical and mental maltreatment in school. Neither children nor parents should have to feel anxious about such things happening. If adults are exposed to maltreatment or persecution, they generally have a good chance of getting help and protection from society. It seems only reasonable that children and young people be guaranteed a corresponding right.

A central subgoal under goal 1 thus includes protecting the whipping boys against harassment and abuse, and guaranteeing them, at the very least, the right to be left in peace. In order to achieve this subgoal, it is important that the bullies' activities be halted or neutralized. In a later section, I will go into more detail about how this can be accomplished.

Perhaps some readers will construe the foregoing as a proposal for inhibiting all kinds of aggressive behavior. This is not my intention. It is obvious that to be able to display a certain amount of aggression—in the sense of behavior that inflicts and/or threatens to inflict injury or discomfort on other individuals (see footnote, p. 17, and Olweus, 1973a)—is a biologically natural and necessary reaction pattern for an individual in terms of survival. For example, to be able to assert oneself forcefully when attacked is from many points of view valuable for the individual and also essential for the continuance of the species. The whipping boy's lack of ability in such "defensive" aggression is certainly a central precondition for becoming a whipping boy. However, this kind of aggression is quite different from that which exists in whipping boy/bully problems. These problems are distinguished primarily by two characteristics: First, there is a clear inequality in relative strength between the aggressors and their targets; and, second, the relationship has a certain degree of stability over time. In my opinion, it is not acceptable that one or more boys repeatedly attack and harass another student who is unable to defend himself effectively. This is not a matter of inhibiting aggression in general, but of taking a stand against maltreatment.

Goal 1 is stated negatively: to limit or prevent whipping boy/bully problems. Goal 2 is more positive: to create better peer relations and especially to create conditions that make it possible for whipping boys and bullies to get along and function better.

Generally, it is a desirable goal for the school to create good peer relations where they do not exist: more friendliness, solidarity, and helpfulness, in brief, a more altruistic attitude (see Bronfenbrenner, 1970). To some degree, this may also have consequences for whipping boy/bully problems. However, it is evident from the analyses in Chapter 5 that good peer relations in a class do not constitute a guarantee against the problems arising. Whipping boy/bully problems can obviously occur in a class that by and large is characterized by good peer relations. In order for the peer group to have a real influence on the problems, certain other more specific reactions seem necessary; I shall come back to this point later on.

As a background for what follows, I shall offer some general reflections on the possibilities for whipping boys and bullies getting along and functioning better. As shown in previous analyses, the whipping boys experienced a good deal of subjective discomfort about their situation: They were anxious, and uncertain of themselves; they had a difficult time at school and frequently felt lonely and left out. Moreover, they were often exposed to attacks. In contrast, the bullies felt secure and unafraid, they had a positive view of themselves, and they were fairly popular with their classmates. However, they were more negative toward their parents, and to some degree toward teachers and school. In spite of these last facts, the bullies gave the decided impression of experiencing no particular subjective discomfort. This, of course, does not preclude the existence of a kind of deep-seated insecurity in at least some of the bullies.

Such an assumption also seems reasonable in view of the probable developmental background of the bullies, as discussed in Chapter 8.

It seems desirable that both bullies and whipping boys function better. By that, I do not mean intellectual performance or similar kinds of performance. For the bullies, functioning better might imply, among other things, that they feel less hostility and react less aggressively to their environment. The possibilities for whipping boys to function better would undoubtedly increase considerably if the bullies' activities were diverted or stopped. Furthermore, it also seems desirable that the whipping boys learn to assert themselves among their peers and to defend themselves with at least some effectiveness; increased self-confidence and less subjective discomfort should be the result. A more positive attitude in at least some of the classmates would also be desirable.

Of course, whipping boys as well as bullies are to be regarded as problem children, and, in entirely different ways, they tend to arouse emotional reactions in the people around them. Whipping boys are often scorned by their peers (and probably by some adults), and they are the object of a kind of pity in many adults. Bullies, on the other hand, often seem to be feared and/or respected by their peers, but they tend to elicit negative and aggressive reactions in adults. Both of these problem groups require concentrated efforts from those around them in order to be able to function better. Perhaps the bullies, in particular, need special help—both for their own and for others' sake.

The prognosis for boys having the kind of problems that characterize the bullies must be regarded as poor. This is evident from Lee Robins's study presented in *Deviant Children Grown Up* (1966). Since I will also have reason to refer to this study later, I will give a brief presentation of selected parts here. The study comprised 524 children who at an average age of 13 years had been referred to a child guidance clinic. All were under 18 when the study took place and had IQ's of 80 or above. Around 75% of the boys were referred to the clinic because of antisocial symptoms or behavior: They were described as being aggressive, ruthless, and relatively free of guilt feelings; they had discipline problems in school and showed behaviors such as truancy and stealing. In the majority of cases, the difficulties could be traced from the ages of 7-8, or approximately from the beginning of school. Around 25% of the children were referred to the clinic because of symptoms that were not antisocial in nature: sleeping and food problems, speech problems, anxiety, shyness, reading and writing difficulties. The study also included a group of 100 matched control children who had not been referred to the clinic.

Thirty years later, in the late 1950s, a follow-up study was conducted on the patients and the control group, who were now between the ages of 40 and 50. One of the many interesting results was that the children with antisocial symptoms showed very poor adjustment as adults: higher frequency of psychiatric illness and a variety of crimes, considerable misuse of alcohol, higher incidence of divorce, social isolation, less professional success, and transfer of adjustment problems to their own children. The more serious antisocial symptoms they had shown as children, the more adjustment problems they displayed as adults. In contrast, the children with symptoms other than antisocial behavior were essentially like the control group in terms of adult adjustment; in certain other respects, however, this group lay somewhere between the antisocial group and the control group.

In this study, lower social groups (blue-collar) were relatively strongly represented, but essentially the same results were found for middle-class children as for children with a poorer socio-economic situation.

Even if there is not a one-to-one relation between Robins's antisocial children and the bullies in the studies presented here—among other things, Robins's group was more hetero-geneous and more seriously disturbed—still, there are obvious points of similarity. Very likely, the bullying behavior is part of a more general antisocial reaction pattern, which not only includes strong aggression against classmates and adults, but also truancy, stealing, and other antisocial activities. Similar symptom patterns have been identified by several different researchers (Bandura & Walters, 1959; Jenkins, 1964; Macfarlane, Allen, & Honzik, 1954; Redl & Wineman, 1957).

The incidence of truancy and stealing has not yet been studied in detail within the present project, but there are reasons for assuming that such behavior has been and will become more frequent in bullies than in boys in general. Preliminary analyses of a follow-up study on 16 bullies, 11 passive whipping boys, and 50 control boys in grade 9 (from the second Solna investigation) provide strong support for such an assumption. A 10-item self-report scale gave very marked results in the expected direction, the bullies reporting much more antisocial activity than the other groups, $p < .001$. Further support is obtained from a recent Swedish study within the context of the Örebro project (Oloffson, 1970; Magnusson, Dunér, & Zetterblom, 1975). This study found a positive relationship between teacher assessments of the boys' aggressiveness toward classmates and teachers in grade 6 and self-reported and actual criminality 3 years later. A clear relationship between frequency of truancy and criminality also appeared. The studies by Lefkowitz, Eron, Walder, and Huesmann (1971) and by West and Farrington (1976) also show that highly aggressive behavior in adolescent boys (around 13 years old) is predictive of later self-reported and actual antisocial behavior. Generally, these studies give a dismal picture of the short-term as well as the long-term prognosis for boys with personality problems of the kind characterizing the bullies.

On the basis of Robins's general results, the prognosis for the whipping boys seems brighter than for the bullies. But the previously cited study by Kagan and Moss (1962) suggests that unless special measures are implemented, the whipping boys may as adults be bothered by inner conflicts and anxiety in social situations. Certain findings in Robins's study (1966, p. 71) are also consistent with such an interpretation. It can be generally assumed, however, that termination of the harassment will increase the likelihood of the whipping boys developing in a positive direction.

FURTHER BACKGROUND FOR REMEDIAL MEASURES

In the previous section, I attempted to show that concentrated efforts are necessary in order to overcome the whipping boy/bully problems in the schools. In my view, the main reasons for change are humanitarian. But even if the problems are seen from an exclusively socioeconomic perspective, the motives for change seem very strong; on the basis of several follow-up studies, it seems very probable that at least a certain percentage of the bullies will cost society considerable amounts of money (e.g., McCord & McCord, 1959; Robins, 1966; West & Farrington, 1976).

In the two goals mentioned above, I have stated my opinion on the direction in which immediate measures ought to proceed. But the important question remains: Which methods should be used?

From the earlier analyses and results, it is evident that measures taken to remedy the whipping boy/bully problems must focus to a considerable extent on modifying the behavior and reaction patterns of the bullies. What kinds of measures, then, are useful or possible? Let us first briefly examine some evidence in the clinical literature.

To my knowledge, no systematic attempts have been made to modify the behavior of bullies, in the sense of the term bully used here. As previously pointed out, however, bullying behavior may be regarded as a component of a more general aggressive antisocial reaction pattern. And there is a good deal of evidence available on the possibility of change in boys with this kind of personality problem. Often, these boys have been aggressive juvenile delinquents and a considerable portion of them very likely could be characterized as bullies, according to the definition in Chapter 4. When evaluating the literature on the treatment of aggressive antisocial males, however, it should be noted that the subjects under treatment have as a rule been more seriously disturbed than the bullies in the present studies and that part of them have displayed other than aggressive disturbances. It should also be emphasized that my central object in examining a selection of studies has been to find some general principles that may serve as guidelines in proposing measures for the modification of the bullies' behavior. It has not been my intent to attempt a complete and balanced review of all the studies conducted in this area.

Perusal of the literature on the treatment of antisocial males shows that a great many studies report fairly discouraging results. With a few exceptions, traditional treatment methods

such as psychoanalysis, psychoanalytically oriented psychotherapy, different kinds of group therapy, client-centered
psychotherapy, and psychodrama have proved to be of little or
questionable worth (see McCord & McCord, 1964; Bender, 1947;
Cleckey, 1964; Hare, 1970). This conclusion seems to apply to
both young people and adults, and also, in considerable measure,
to children. The results of Robins's study (1966) also suggest
that clinical treatment had insignificant effects. Robins points
out that the treatment efforts in her study had been of a fairly
primitive and sporadic nature, but several other projects have
shown that more modern social work methods (such as casework
and counseling) have hardly been more successful in preventing
or "postponing" antisocial behavior (McCord & McCord, 1959;
Powers & Witmer, 1950; Tait & Hodges, 1962). As with many
other kinds of disturbances, a certain ("spontaneous") improvement can occur over the years. However, such changes seem to
appear late in life (if they happen at all)—in Robins's antisocial
group, about a third of the subjects improved in this way,
generally between the ages of 30 and 40.

It is scarcely surprising that the treatment techniques mentioned above have not been particularly successful. The desirable
prerequisites for such treatment are usually missing: among
other things, that the patient experiences his disturbance as
unpleasant or burdensome and wishes to change his behavior.
That the majority of bullies would not be highly motivated to
engage in this kind of treatment is evident from their view of
themselves (confirmed by their mothers' views; see Chapter 7).

The general picture of the treatment results achieved by a
number of different techniques is thus fairly gloomy. However,
some studies of milieu therapy within the context of an
institution have reported results that seem somewhat more
promising. For example, Craft, Stephenson, and Granger (1964)
compared the effects of two kinds of institutional treatment on
50 mainly antisocial patients between the ages of 13 and 25.
Two different treatment programs were used. One group of
patients lived in a very tolerant institutional climate and took
part in intensive group therapy: the other program was much
more "authoritarian" and consisted of a firm but friendly form
of discipline and only superficial individual therapy. At their

discharge after 1 year, none of the subject groups showed marked signs of change in personality or adjustment, according to psychological tests. Nevertheless, approximately 1 year after dismissal there were clear differences between the groups in terms of the number of crimes committed and convictions obtained. The researchers concluded that work training in a friendly but disciplined institutional atmosphere probably has a better effect on this kind of problem than work training combined with group therapy in a permissive institutional climate.

Other institutions have also reported some progress with fairly authoritarian methods, often combined with intensive follow-up treatment (see Hare, 1970). Factors considered to be of importance for successful treatment results include a positive attachment to an adult and the existence of discreet but powerful social control exerted not only by adults, but also by leaders among the boys themselves (McCord & McCord, 1964). Related factors such as strong group pressure directed toward more social behavior have been emphasized by others (Arendsen Hein, 1959).

Robins found very little that could explain why positive changes occurred when they did occur. Her tentative conclusion on this point is that increased social control is necessary for improvement, a conclusion that is in general agreement with what has been reported above. Among other things, Robins proposes closer supervision of the spare time of children with early antisocial tendencies. In this connection, it has been shown that inadequate parental supervision of a sons's spare time, and especially of his activities in the evening, is clearly related to his tendency to commit crimes (e.g., Dinitz, Scarpitti, & Reckless, 1962; Olofsson, 1971).

It should be mentioned that the modification of antisocial behavior in young males is a rapidly expanding field, and many new techniques are being tried out. Several of these techniques are based on behavior modification (see, e.g., Burchard & Harig, 1976; Davidson & Seidman, 1974) and/or modeling principles (see, e.g., Bandura, 1973; Sarason & Ganzer, 1973). Although follow-up data on the persistence of treatment effects are often lacking, it seems fair to conclude that several recent studies have reported rather promising results, providing grounds for a somewhat more optimistic view of the changeability of antisocial behavior in adolescent males. No doubt, additional suggestions and guidelines for the modification of bullies may be derived from these studies.

Before suggesting a few general conclusions, however, the extensive work carried out by Gerald Patterson and his associates at Oregon Research Institute should be briefly presented. This work has been described in a number of papers and book chapters, in two programmed texts, and in a manual (for references, see, e.g., Patterson, 1975; Patterson, Reid, Jones, & Conger, 1975). In a recent publication, Patterson (1975) gives an overview of the project, the Social Learning Project, and some of the results obtained. The basic subject group consisted of 27 families with at least 1 boy between the ages of 5 and 15 (median age = 7 years) who had been identified as a severe "conduct problem." Approximately 60% of the boys were highly aggressive (at home), and a good deal of them displayed maladaptive behavior in school, including academic failure. The families had been referred to the Social Learning Project mainly by different community agencies such as mental hygiene clinics, schools, and the Juvenile Court. Although the Oregon sample of boys was younger than the bullies in the present studies and also included a number of boys with problems other than aggressive behavior, it seems reasonable to assume that a considerable portion of the Oregon boys could be characterized as bullies or potential bullies in the sense used here.

Each of the 27 families was treated with the family intervention program developed at the Oregon Research Institute. This program, which includes several steps, focuses on teaching the parents more adequate child management skills. An essential component of the program is to teach the parents to use rewards (social or nonsocial) consistently for adequate behaviors on the part of the boy and mildly aversive consequences (e.g., time-out or loss of privileges) for maladaptive ("deviant") behaviors.

At the end of the treatment period, there were considerable changes in the behaviors of the problem children. Approximately two-thirds to three-fourths of the boys showed major reductions in maladaptive behaviors from pretreatment (baseline) levels. The average reduction in maladaptive behavior was approximately 50%, as measured by the behavioral coding system used in the Social Learning Project, and a substantial number of boys were functioning within what had been defined as "normal" ranges. Follow-up data collected on a subsample of the families (unfortunately only 17 of the 27 families participated in the follow-up) a year after treatment termination showed that the intervention effects tended to be lasting, at least for the subset of the sample studied. In Patterson's words, "The follow-up data provided modest support for the notion that the changes persisted" (1975, p. 306). It should be noted that the family intervention program required an average of only 32 hours of professional time per family.

Although a more definite evaluation of the persistence of effects of the Oregon family intervention program has to await further and more comprehensive follow-up data, this project shows that it is possible, with a limited amount of professional time, to produce important reductions in maladaptive behaviors in a substantial portion of boys with "conduct problems." When trying to extract in nontechnical language the treatment elements and processes responsible for the relatively successful outcome, the following appear particularly important, in my interpretation (see also Patterson, 1975). The intervention program introduces some order and consistency in a disrupted family system characterized by frequent conflicts, inconsistency, and use of power-assertive disciplinary techniques. At first, the boy experiences the new limits set by the parents as frustrations, but gradually he will accept them and maybe even find them a relief. Most important, the parental techniques for enforcing the restrictions and rules include only mildly aversive consequences, which thus entails a reduction or elimination of physical abuse previously used by many of the parents. In addition, the consistent use of rewards in the form of praise, attention, and concrete benefits for prosocial behaviors in the boy makes the boy feel more accepted and liked by his parents. At the same time, the decrease in the boy's aggressive outbursts and other maladaptive behaviors reduces frustration and hostility in the parents and makes them perceive the boy in a more appreciative way. In other words, a number of positive processes are initiated that gradually result in more mutually satisfying parent-child interactions. In successful cases, which I assume to be the ones in which the parent(s) has some genuine basic interest in the child, the newly established interaction system may become relatively stable.

When considering the results obtained within the Social Learning Project, it should be noted that the age of the treated boys was lower than that of the bullies in the present studies (median age = 13 years as compared to 7 years in the Oregon sample). The parents' potential for influencing a child around 7 years old is normally fairly great. As is well known, however, the parental influence gradually decreases as the child grows older and extrafamilial influences such as those from the peer group come to play a successively greater role. Accordingly, when considering remedial measures for adolescent and pre-adolescent bullies, the peer group must be assigned important functions (see also Bronfenbrenner, 1970; Staub, 1971). This conclusion receives additional support from the finding that treatment effects obtained in the home setting do not automatically generalize to other settings such as the school (Burchard & Harig, 1976; Patterson, 1975; Wahler, 1969). If bullying behavior in the school setting is to be modified, it is thus natural that peers, teachers, and other personnel in the school play a crucial part in the remedial program. It may be noted in passing that the fact that treatment effects appear to be fairly specific to the setting has been recognized at an early stage in the Social Learning Project: In case a boy displays maladaptive behavior in both the school and the home settings, a particular school intervention program involving the teacher and the peers is implemented in addition to the ordinary family training program (Patterson, 1975).

A few general conclusions can be derived from this admittedly sketchy review. First, there seems to be substantial agreement among clinicians and researchers that it is difficult to achieve positive changes in aggressive antisocial boys (and adults). The younger the boy when remedial measures are initiated, the greater the chances for enduring improvement. Furthermore, the studies in which some treatment progress has been demonstrated suggest the following conclusion: There is a need for increased social control, preferably exerted by both adults and peers. This control should be at the same time friendly, determined, and consistent.

In this context, it is of interest that scarcely any of the studies examined indicate that a generally permissive attitude is useful for these kinds of problems. On the contrary, it appears that a very tolerant attitude and negligible supervision on the part of adults are factors that directly contribute to antisocial behavior in the young. It is quite possible that such adult attitudes toward the boys may be interpreted as an expression of indifference toward what they do (see Bronfenbrenner, 1970).

It would be possible to explain in more technical language that the above conclusions are very reasonable from theoretical points of view. That, however, is beyond the scope of this book. Here, I will content myself with emphasizing that the treatment results discussed are not surprising in view of the personality structure and background experiences found in boys with aggressive antisocial reaction patterns. It is very probable that a hostile punitive control would lead to strong direct opposition, and to at least indirectly destructive acts on the part of the bullies. A determined and consistent but basically positive and supportive (authoritative)[1] attitude will certainly also elicit quite

---

[1] In some quarters, suggestions of even a slightly controlling character seem to be regarded as manifestations of "authoritarianism." To some extent, this may be due to the frequently cited studied by Kurt Lewin and his associates (Lewin, Lippitt, & White, 1939; White & Lippitt, 1960) on the effects of different leadership styles. The authoritarian leader in the Lewin experiments was not only controlling; he was also characterized by a cold, hostile, and critical attitude. However, control may be combined with a friendly and supportive attitude (see Chapter 8). There is thus no reason to make control synonymous with the negatively loaded concept of authoritarianism. And there is, in fact, a good deal of research indicating that determined *and* warm control exerted by parents is likely to contribute to the development of a number of socially valued qualities, such as independence and high self-esteem (see e.g., Mussen, Conger, & Kagan, 1969). I would like to suggest in passing that the conclusions derived from these early studies by Lewin and his associates be regarded with great skepticism (cf. the generally noncritical presentation in textbooks). In my view, they are beset by so many methodological weaknesses that it is doubtful that they permit any conclusions at all (see also Sechrest, 1964).

a bit of aggression and protest, but gradually it may serve as a limit and support, without causing much provocation.

I also want to emphasize that the program of change to be discussed in the following sections consists of a set of co-ordinated actions on the part of the school authorities, the teachers, the school psychologists and social workers, the pupils, and the parents. In the main, it is based on a utilization of the existing social environment of the boys. In its general outline, it is not "individual-centered," though particular treatment pro-grams may be necessary for boys with especially serious prob-lems.

As mentioned earlier, I have chosen not to propose remedial measures in concrete detail. The reason for this is that it is very difficult, if not impossible, to discuss remedial measures on a specific level without committing oneself to a particular theo-retical perspective or a particular "treatment school." Since it is my conviction that the problems under consideration may be successfully tackled from several different angles, I consider it appropriate to restrict myself to suggesting some central guiding lines rather than presenting specific proposals. On the basis of these guidelines and the particular theoretical perspective adopted, more concrete remedial measures may be constructed.

GENERAL MEASURES
FOR ACHIEVING THE LIMITING GOAL

The conclusions derived from the previous analyses can now be combined with the two goals for immediate action. The first goal can perhaps be described as *the limiting goal*, and the second as the *integrating goal*. It is important that a program of change is designed in such a way that both these goals are attended to. In the following, I will discuss them separately, though the boundaries between them are fluid at times.

The limiting goal entails a clear repudiation of repeated physical and mental maltreatment. Naturally, this repudiation should be directed primarily against the phenomenon, not the particular bully; but it seems inevitable that it will also affect the bully to some degree. Such an emphasis ought to come from many different sources: from the school authorities—

admonitions that physical and mental abuse will not be tolerated in the school; from the teachers—clear statements and, in addition, active intervention in situations where mobbing occurs or can be suspected to occur; from the classmates—active intervention, too, with the aim of protecting the whipping boy; from the parents of bullies—through serious discussions, but not physical punishment. Even though the peer group very likely can play an important role, I believe that the adults, at least at first, must assume the main responsibility for stressing such a repudiation. This requires a certain amount of courage on the part of the adults, especially since all suggestions of even a slightly controlling character have come to seem so unfashionable (see footnote 1, p. 183). However, *to fail to stop these activities implies a tacit confirmation—an attitude that seems very inhumane.*

But can't a general repudiation of bullying involve the bullies in further conflicts with society? Isn't there a large danger of what are usually called *stigmatization effects*? The concept of stigmatization implies that the intervention by adults and society, the "labeling" of an individual who deviates from social norms, actively interferes with his adjustment, and directly works against their purpose. Here, I will make only brief reference to some pertinent results from two previously cited studies.

In Olofsson's study (1971), the following comparison was carried out. One group consisted of boys who had committed a particular criminal act, been reported to the police, and referred to a Child Welfare Committee; the other group was composed of boys who had committed the same offense, been discovered, but had not been reported to the police or treated by other agencies. By the end of the ninth grade, no differences could be found in the degree of self-reported criminality of the two groups. There was nothing in the results supporting the idea that the activities of the Child Welfare Committee and the police had stigmatizing effects (p. 259). A similar conclusion emerges from Robins's material (1966) on the effects of being referred to a child guidance clinic. What appeared to create the problems later in life was primarily the nature and severity of the childhood behavior that had occasioned the referral. There was no indication that being labeled as a "problem child" had a stigmatizing effect (p. 293).

These results indicate that the risks of negative effects resulting from measures taken by adults and society can often be exaggerated (see also Gove, 1975). In addition, the suggested repudiation of bullying would have a considerably less official nature than, for instance, formal treatment in a Child Welfare Committee. Furthermore, this kind of limiting measure must be supplemented by measures directed toward the integrating goal, as mentioned earlier.

In the light of the previous considerations, I think it is of very great importance that the school authorities make some form of official declaration against the phenomenon; this would be of central importance for teachers, parents, students, and all others who are involved in the problems.

As mentioned, the peer group should be able to play a significant role in limiting and preventing whipping boy/bully problems. I am convinced that there often are students in a class who actually dislike the bully's behavior toward the whipping boy, but who do not intervene for one or several of the following reasons: The bully is strong and frightening, and he may have rough boys supporting him; the whipping boy is not popular; and there is an implicit rule that everybody should manage his own affairs. To some extent, it should be possible to overcome these obstacles to intervention with the help of adults who encourage the development of a generally negative attitude toward mobbing—a group morale that takes a stand against physical and mental maltreatment. A conceivable consequence of this might be that the students in at least the higher classes elect a couple of calm, strong boys who would have the task of intervening in harassment that occurs during class breaks and other occasions. The whipping boys might find it easier to turn to such special representatives than to teachers and parents. Clearly, there are a great many good and constructive resources in the classes—however, it is a matter of getting these resources activated and coordinated. The students and their organizations should be able to make very meaningful contributions in co-operation with the school personnel. I imagine that the students themselves, who in some ways know the problem best, should be able to offer suitable proposals and solutions within the context of the stated goals.

It is natural to wonder if building up more effective protection for the whipping boys is going to create an artificial situation that will impede their adjustment to the peer group. I do not think the risks are great, especially since the whipping boy's status in the group is so low—accordingly, it cannot become much poorer. In addition, there should very likely be a beneficial effect on the whipping boy's development if he can be relatively sure of avoiding open harassment. This would certainly make it easier for the whipping boy to make peer contacts. In this connection, I also want to emphasize how important it is that parents who know or suspect that their children are whipping boys get in touch with the main teacher. It is unwise to try to escape the problem by assuming that the students themselves will clear up the situation.

GENERAL MEASURES
FOR ACHIEVING THE INTEGRATING GOAL

I will now briefly discuss the main points in the part of the program directed toward the integrating goal.

First, I would like to emphasize the importance of intensifying contact between the school and the home. In order to achieve student care that is worthy of the name, there must be closer and more trusting relationships between the main teacher and the parents than are commonly the case. It is, of course, very difficult to take up a question as sensitive and complicated as whipping boy/bully problems if the main teacher meets the parents only once or twice a year, and then often in large groups. However, building up closer contact requires considerable time and effort on the part of the teacher. This has been shown, for instance, in the Pedo Project at the Tunaberg School in Uppsala, where different methods have been tried for creating better relationships between main teachers, parents, and students (unpublished paper). In this area, there should be opportunities for quite a bit of experimentation. In my opinion, a very important part of the main teacher's job is the time devoted to student care, especially in terms of the present problem. It

seems necessary that a larger part of the teacher's working time
be used for this kind of activity than is common today;
naturally, it is also reasonable that the teachers be compensated
either by a reduction of teaching duties or in some other way.

Even where such possibilities and established routines do not
exist, this should not keep the main teachers from working
energetically to make satisfactory contacts with the parents of
problem children in particular. It is probable that the initiative
here—at least with regard to the parents of the bullies—will have
to be taken by the teachers, since it is known that parents of
children with antisocial tendencies often stay away from parent
meetings and class visits (Olofsson, 1971). Some of the problems
that the main teachers may encounter in this connection are
surely of such complexity that the help of a special consultant
may be necessary. I will come back to this question later.

Another main point in an integrating program is that adults
must commit themselves to participating more actively in the
lives of children and young peope. Bronfenbrenner (1970)
presents data and experiences indicating that a marked age
segregation is developing; parents are together with their children
to a steadily declining extent, and the vacuum that arises is
filled by the peer group. It seems quite clear to Bronfenbrenner
that such a development leads to unfortunate consequences:
increased violence, indifference, and alienation of the younger
generation from all layers of society. In this connection, it is
particularly interesting that there seems to be some ambivalence
among the young people toward their own increasing association
with the peer group. The children who were strongly peer-
oriented in Bronfenbrenner's study (sixth grade) seemed to have
become this way because of parental indifference rather than
attraction to the peer group. As might be expected, the predominantly peer-oriented children devoted themselves to a
greater extent than adult-oriented children to antisocial activities
such as "doing something illegal," playing hookey, and teasing
other children. The general conclusion of Bronfenbrenner's
analysis is that the adults must engage themselves more actively
in the lives of children and young people. But how can this be
accomplished?

As far as the individual family is concerned, it is essential that the parents realize the importance of spending time and involving themselves with their child or children. Naturally, the form of the relationship will vary with the conditions, but it is important that parents see the building up of close contact with their children as a significant task. Of course, young people need relationships with peers as a link in the development of independence, but it is clear that there is both need and desire on the part of many young people to have closer ties with adults. There should not have to be a sharp division into different cultures according to principles of age. Without going into more detail here, I want to emphasize the general importance of establishing close relationships as early in the child's life as possible; this no doubt would prevent the development of many crises in adolescence.

Changes in the individual family are not the only way to create better relationships between the generations. Adults could certainly exert considerably greater efforts toward finding meaningful recreational activities that involve both children and adults. In addition to governmental and community authorities (via local recreational organizations, for example), parent associations such as the P.T.A. can play an important role. There are many possibilities: football or ice hockey played by both parents and children, family activities at the school on weekends, and so on. To a greater extent than is now the case, workshop teachers and former athletes could be used to lead different recreational activities for young and old. The list of imaginable proposals could be made considerably longer, but the important thing is that activities be sought that involve closer and more pleasurable contact between younger and older generations. It would certainly be very valuable if some of these activities could occur at the school; this might lead to more natural and relaxed attitudes toward the school on the part of both parents and children. For children with emotionally unsatisfying home relationships, this kind of contact could also have beneficial effects because of the association with adult "models" who have a clear prosocial identification. Such positive ties should have special value for the bullies.

Naturally, the teacher has a central role in an integrating program of change. I have already stressed the importance of establishing closer cooperation with the students' parents. But the teacher also has the very important duty of activating the positive forces in the class and helping the bullies and whipping boys to find more appropriate kinds of reaction patterns. Perhaps the bullies' energy, physical strength, and strong need to dominate could be utilized in a more constructive way, through forceful self-assertion within a system of rules that limits its destructive aspects, for example, football and ice hockey. Furthermore, it is very likely that consistent praise and encouragement for socially acceptable behaviors will be valuable, at least for aggressive children of lower ages (Bandura, 1973). On the other hand, the whipping boys need support and encouragement to strengthen their low self-esteem, as well as direct training in "defensive" aggression (assertive training): It is desirable that they be able to assert themselves with some force if attacked or, at least, that they not be afraid to react strongly in one way or another. Some parents and fellow victims advise the whipping boy not to worry about the harassment and not to try fighting back, but this seems to be an unwise strategy. The whipping boy's chances of defending himself effectively in a fight with a bully are usually not very great, but the mere occurrence of a vehement emotional reaction to the bullying is likely to have a restraining effect in many instances. In any case, it is obvious that passive, evasive behavior does not prevent mobbing (see Chapter 7). In this context, it should be generally emphasized that measures taken to "integrate" bullies and whipping boys will probably be rather ineffective if they are not firmly supported by the limiting measures mentioned earlier.

As I have suggested above, some of the problems are so complicated that the teachers, who normally do not have training in psychotherapy or mental hygiene, need the help of specially trained consultants. Such help can take several forms: Discussion groups for teachers can be formed that meet regularly under the direction of a specially trained leader (consultant) in order to discuss different class problems, particularly whipping boy/bully problems; in more difficult cases, the consultant and the main teacher can talk with the student and his parents in order to develop an individually designed program that may also involve contact with personnel from a child guidance clinic; the consultant and the main teacher can initiate class discussions of interpersonal problems, particularly from the present point of view (such discussions could use, for example, plays, films, or role playing as a point of departure). All of these kinds of special measures are already being tried in some Swedish communities, and they seem to be valuable forms of activity.

It appears natural that the school psychologists engage themselves in such consulting duties. However, it is likely that they will require special training for at least some of the measures mentioned. The same can be said about the school social workers. It seems unlikely that these two groups of personnel would have sufficient time to assume complete responsibility for such consultant functions, in addition to their ordinary duties in the school. It is possible that for certain problems, help could be obtained from the personnel of a child guidance clinic. This could contribute to closer contact between these institutions and the school, which I think would be valuable from many viewpoints. Certain difficult cases, particularly if discovered early, might benefit from an individually designed treatment program; but very few school psychologists have time to incorporate this kind of effort into their work program.

In the previous sections, I have attempted to present some central guidelines for a coherent program of action based on the goals stated and research results on the nature of the problem. Further proposals such as assigning special duties to recess teachers and using special instruction in particular cases, could be formulated within the framework of the principal guidelines. However, I will not tire the reader by presenting additional points of view on these issues; a number of proposals will certainly emerge if a program of change is initiated following the general lines of direction stated.

PREVENTIVE MEASURES

Many of the measures discussed in the previous account can be considered preventive in nature; if there is a coordinated program of measures, the possibilities are probably good for combatting tendencies toward maladjustment that manifest themselves in early grades, for example. But as was evident from the research results presented in Chapter 8, it is very likely that the basis for whipping boy/bully problems is laid before the child begins school. This fact must lead to a consideration of questions involving the early care of children and general attitudes about the kind of parental and peer relationships that are necessary for an adequate development of a child. A number of answers to these questions will indirectly be evident from the research described earlier. I will return to these questions in later reports.

APPENDIX

Statements in the Q sort and the Q inventory. The number refers to the order in which the items were presented. R = reversed scoring (factor scales). (See discussion of Q sort and Q inventory on pp. 96–117.)

Factor scale I = *Feelings of maladjustment and inadequacy* (12 items)
Factor scale II = *Aggression* (11 items)
Factor scale III = *Self-confidence* (independence, toughness; 10 items)
Factor scale IV = *Closeness to parents* (10 items)

A PRIORI DIMENSION:
AGGRESSION AND VIOLENCE (19 ITEMS)

	Factor scale	Factor loading
3. I often tease other boys.	II	.46
5. I often fight with other boys.	II	.59
6. I often think it is fun to make trouble.	II	.60
9. In general, I think getting angry doesn't pay.(R)	II	.38

193

	Factor scale	Factor loading
14. I am glad when people say I am well brought up.	IV	.52
18. I think it is better to be quiet than to make a fuss if somebody is unpleasant. (R)	II	.60
22. Usually I don't get angry if somebody teases me. (R)	II	.42
26. When I have had a disagreement with a teacher, I tend to have a bad conscience afterwards.		
31. I am often angry with myself for acting stupidly.	IV	.55
32. I think a boy should be able to take a few knocks.	III	.46
35. When a boy teases me, I try to give him a good beating.	II	.60
37. If I get angry, I usually don't show it. (R)	II	.40
39. If a teacher has promised we'll have some fun but then changes his mind, I protest strongly.	III	.39
41. I get angry with other people easily.	II	.42
43. When an adult is grouchy toward me, I make an effort to be extra friendly.	IV	.54
44. I prefer to get out of the way then somebody is picking on me. (R)	II	.61
51. When an adult is annoyed with me, I usually feel that I am at fault.		
55. I think fighting is silly. (R)	II	.57
57. When a teacher criticizes me, I tend to answer back and protest.	III	.40

A PRIORI DIMENSION: ANXIETY (7 ITEMS)

13. I seldom worry about things.	III	.43
16. It usually takes a long time for me to adjust to something new.		

	Factor scale	Factor loading
20. I find it difficult to speak up in class.	I	.39
28. I am usually fairly brave.	III	.54
33. I am often afraid of getting sick.		
40. I am usually uneasy when I am home alone.		
45. I am often afraid that something unplesant will happen to me.	I	.45

A PRIORI DIMENSION:
SELF-ESTEEM (9 ITEMS)

8. I often find my situation difficult and troublesome.	I	.71
10. I often feel lonely and neglected at school.	I	.61
15. I can almost always look out for myself.	III	.54
24. Generally, I am fairly sure of myself.	III	.56
29. Things always seem to be going wrong for me.	I	.73
38. I give up quite easily.	I	.43
48. Usually, it is easy for me to make up my mind.	III	.53
52. In general, I am satisfied with myself.	III	.37
56. I often feel like a failure.	I	.71

A PRIORI DIMENSION:
IDENTIFICATION (10 ITEMS)

2. I prefer to be with boys who are older than I am		
11. I have often wanted to be someone else.	I	.55
17. I prefer to be with boys who are younger than I am.	I	.38
21. I often have fun with my father.		

	Factor scale	Factor loading
25. I don't think there are great differences between boys and girls		
34. I would like to change many things about myself.	I	.59
36. I often wish I were younger.	I	.43
46. When I grow up, I want to be like my father.	IV	.37
47. I would rather be with adults than boys my own age.		
49. Now and then I have almost wished I were a girl.	I	.48

A PRIORI DIMENSION:
CLOSENESS TO PARENTS (8 ITEMS)

7. My mother and father make many decisions for me.	IV	.39
12. My mother often tells me to be careful when I am out.	IV	.44
23. I think it is best for children if their parents make decisions for them.	IV	.62
27. I nearly always tell my mother what I have been doing.	IV	.53
30. It is often nice not to have to make decisions for myself.	IV	.61
42. I have wanted to run away from home several times.		
50. My mother lets me stay home from school whenever I feel tired or out of sorts.		
53. I like to have a grown-up around.	IV	.48

REMAINING ITEMS (4 ITEMS)

4. I prefer to have the same kind of clothes as the other boys.

	Factor scale	Factor loading

54. I often do what I want without
    bothering about what other
    people think.   III   .39
 1. I often read books in my free
    time. (filler item)
19. I think it is fun to play ice hockey.
    (filler item)

REFERENCES

Allen, G. J., Chinsky, J. M., Larcen, S. W., Lochman, J. E., & Selinger, H. V. *Community psychology and the schools.* Hillsdale, N.J.: Lawrence Erlbaum Associates, 1976.

Allport, F. H. *Social psychology.* Boston: Houghton Mifflin, 1924.

Arendsen Hein, G. Group therapy with criminal psychopaths. *Acta Psychoterapeutica,* Supplement, 1959, *7,* 6–16.

Armstrong, J. S., & Soelberg, P. On the interpretation of factor analysis. *Psychological Bulletin,* 1968, *70,* 361–364.

Ausubel, D. P. *Educational psychology: A cognitive view.* New York: Holt, Rinehart and Winston, 1968.

Baird, L. L. Big school, small school: A critical examination of the hypothesis. *Journal of Educational Psychology,* 1969, *60,* 253–259.

Bandura, A. *Aggression: A social learning analysis.* Englewood Cliffs, N.J.: Prentice-Hall, 1973.

Bandura, A., & Walters, R. H. *Adolescent aggression.* New York: Ronald Press, 1959.

Barker, R. G., & Gump, P. V. *Big school, small school.* Stanford, Calif.: Stanford University Press, 1964.

Becker, W. C. Developmental psychology. *Annual Review of Psychology,* 1962, *13,* 1–34.

Becker, W. C. Consequences of different kinds of parental

discipline. In M. L. Hoffman & L. W. Hoffman (Eds.), *Review of child development research* (Vol. 1). New York: Russell Sage, 1964.

Bell, R. A. A reinterpretation of the direction of effects in studies of socialization. *Psychological Review*, 1968, *75*, 81–95.

Bell, R. A. Stimulus control of parent or caretaker behavior by off-spring. *Developmental Psychology*, 1971, *4*, 63–72.

Bender, L. Psychopathic behavior disorders in children. In R. Lindner & R. Seliger (Eds.), *Handbook of correctional psychology*. New York: Philosophical Library, 1947.

Bennis, W. G., Benne, K. D., & Chin, R. (Eds.). *The planning of change*. New York: Holt, Rinehart and Winston, 1976.

Berkowitz, L. *Aggression: A social psychological analysis*. New York: McGraw-Hill, 1962.

Berkowitz, L. The concept of aggressive drive: Some additional considerations. In L. Berkowitz (Ed.), *Advances in experimental social psychology* (Vol. 2). New York: Academic Press, 1965.

Block, J. *The Q-sort method in personality assessment and psychatric research*. Springfield, Ill.: Charles C Thomas, 1961.

Block, J. The equivalence of measures and the correction for attenuation. *Psychological Bulletin*, 1963, *60*, 152–156.

Block, J. *Lives through time*. Berkeley, Calif.: Bancroft Books, 1971.

Boalt, G., & Husén, T. *Skolans sociologi*. Stockholm: Almqvist & Wiksell, 1967.

Bowers, K. S. Situationism in psychology: An analysis and a critique. *Psychological Review*, 1973, *80*, 307–336.

Bronfenbrenner, U. *Two words of childhood: U.S. and U.S.S.R.* New York: Russell Sage, 1970.

Burchard, J. D., & Harig, P. T. Behavior modification and juvenile delinquency. In H. Leitenberg (Ed.), *Handbook of behavior modification*. New York: Prentice-Hall, 1976.

Cartwright, D., & Zander, A. F. (Eds.). *Group dynamics: Research and theory*. New York: Harper & Row, 1968.

Cattell, R. B., Blewett, D. B., & Beloff, J. R. The inheritance of personality. A multiple variance analysis determination of approximate nature-nurture ratios for primary personality factors in Q-data. *American Journal of Human Genetics*, 1955, *7*, 122–146.

Clark, F. W., Evans, D. R., & Hamerlynck, L. A. (Eds.). *Implementing behavioral programs for schools and clinics.* Champaign, Ill.: Research Press, 1972.

Checkley, H. *The mask of sanity.* St. Louis: Mosby, 1964.

Cohen, R. Some statistical issues in psychological research. In B. B. Wolman (Ed.). *Handbook of clinical psychology.* New York: McGraw-Hill, 1965.

Comstock, G. A., & Rubinstein, E. A. (Eds.). *Television and social behavior* (Vol. 1). Washington, D.C.: U.S. Government Printing Office, 1971.

Cowen, E. L. Social and community interventions. *Annual Review of Psychology*, 1973, *24*, 423–472.

Craft, M., Stephenson, G., & Granger, C. A controlled trial of authoritarian and self-governing regimes with adolescent psychopaths. *American Journal of Orthopsychiatry*, 1964, *34*, 543–554.

Cronbach, L. J. *Essentials of psychological testing.* New York: Harper & Row, 1970.

Davidson, W. S., & Seidman, E. Studies of behavior modiciation and juvenile delinquency. *Psychological Bulletin*, 1974, *81*, 998–1011.

DeVore, I. (Ed.). *Primate behavior.* New York: Holt, Rinehart and Winston, 1965.

DeVore, I. Primate behavior. In *International encyclopedia of the social sciences.* New York: Crowell, Collier and Macmillan, 1968.

Dinitz, S., Scarpitti, F. R., & Reckless, W. C. Delinquency vulnerability: A cross group and longitudinal analysis. *American Sociological Review*, 1962, *27*, 517–522.

Eaves, L., & Eysenck, H. The nature of extraversion: A genetical analysis. *Journal of Personality and Social Psychology*, 1975, *32*, 102–112.

Eron, L. D., Huesmann, L. R., Lefkowitz, M. M., & Walder, L. O. Does television violence cause aggression? *American Psychologist*, 1972, *27*, 253–263.

Eron, L. D., Walder, L. O., & Lefkowitz, M. M. *Learning of aggression in children.* Boston: Little, Brown, 1971.

Feshbach, S. Aggression. In P. H. Mussen (Ed.), *Carmichael's manual of child psychology* (3rd ed., Vol. 2). New York: Wiley, 1970.

Goldinger, B., & Mellis, I. *Undersökning angående utländska barns skolanpassning inom Solna grundskolor.* Unpublished paper, 1970.

Gove, W. R. (Ed.). *The labelling of deviance: Evaluating a perspective.* Beverley Hills, Calif.: Sage, 1975.

Hamburg, D. A. Aggressive behavior of chimpanzees and baboons in natural habitats. *Journal of Psychiatric Research,* 1971, *8,* 385-398.

Hare, R. D. *Psychopathy: Theory and research.* New York: Wiley, 1970.

Hartmann, E., Kris, E., & Loewenstein, R. M. Notes on the theory of aggression. *Psychoanalytic study of the child* (Vols. 3-4). New York: International Universities Press, 1949.

Hartup, W. W. Peer interaction and social organization. In P. H. Mussen (Ed.), *Carmichael's manual of child psychology* (3rd ed., Vol. 2). New York: Wiley, 1970.

Hays, W. L. *Statistics for psychologists.* New York: Holt, Rinehart and Winston, 1973.

Heinemann, P.-P. *Mobbning—gruppvåld bland barn och vuxna.* Stockholm: Natur och Kultur, 1972.

Heise, D. R. The heritability of personality. In D. R. Heise (Ed.), *Personality: Biosocial bases.* New York: Rand McNally, 1973.

Jenkins, R. L. Diagnosis, dynamics and treatment in child psychiatry. *Psychiatric Research Reports,* 1964, *18,* 91-120.

Jersild, A. T., & Markey, F. V. Conflicts between preschool children. *Child Development Monograph,* 1935, *21.*

Jinks, J. L., & Fulker, D. W. A comparison of the bio-metrical, genetical, MAVA, and classical approaches to the analysis of human behavior. *Psychological Bulletin,* 1970, *73* 311-349.

Johanneson, I. Ett attitydformulär för studium av elevernas innställning till skolmiljön. *Rapport från pedagogisk-*

psykologiska institutionen, Lärarhögskolan i Stockholm, 1966.

Jöreskog, K. G. *Statistical estimation in factor analysis.* Uppsala: Almqvist & Wiksell, 1963.

Kagan, J., & Moss, H. *Birth to maturity: A study in psychological development.* New York: Wiley, 1962.

Kaiser, H. F. Computer program for varimax rotation in factor analysis. *Educational and Psychological Measurement,* 1959, *19,* 413–420.

Klackenberg, G. *A prospective longitudinal study of children. Acta Paediatrica,* Suppl. *224,* 1971.

Kluckhorn, C., & Murray, H. A. *Personality in nature, society and culture.* New York: Knopf, 1961.

Kragh, U. The Defence Mechanism Test: A new method for diagnosis and personnel selection. *Journal of Applied Psychology,* 1960, *44,* 303–309.

Kragh, U. *Defence Mechanism Test.* Manual. Stockholm: Skandinaviska Testförlaget, 1969.

Lefkowitz, M. M., Eron, L. D., Walder, L. O., & Huesmann, L. R. Television violence and child aggression: A follow-up study. In G. A. Comstock & E. A. Rubinstein (Eds.), *Television and social behavior* (Vol. 3). Washington, D.C.: U.S. Government Printing Office, 1971.

Lewin, K. *Principles of topological psychology.* New York: 1936.

Lewin, K., Lippitt, R., & White, R. K. Patterns of aggressive behavior in experimentally created "social climates." *Journal of Social Psychology,* 1939, *10,* 271–299.

Lindzey, G. (Ed.). *Handbook of social psychology* (Vol. 1). Cambridge, Mass.: Addison-Wesley, 1954.

Lord, F. M., & Novick, M. R. *Statistical theories of mental test scores.* Reading, Mass.: Addison-Wesley, 1968.

Lorenz, K. *On aggression.* New York: Bantam Books, 1966.

Maccoby, E. E., & Jacklin, C. N. *The psychology of sex differences.* Palo Alto: Stanford University Press, 1974.

Macfarlane, J. W., Allen, L., & Honzik, M. P. *A developmental study of the behavior problems of normal children between 21 months and 14 years.* Los Angeles: University of California Press, 1954.

Magnusson, D., Dunér, A., Zetterblom, G. *Adjustment: A longitudinal study.* Uppsala: Almqvist & Wiksell, 1975.

McCord, W., & McCord, J. *Origins of crime.* New York: Columbia University Press, 1959.

McCord, W., & McCord, J. *The psychopath: An essay on the criminal mind.* New York: Van Nostrand, 1964.

McCord, W., McCord, J., & Howard, A. Familial correlates of aggression in nondelinquent male children. *Journal of Abnormal and Social Psychology,* 1961, *62,* 79–93.

McNemar, Q. *Psychological statistics.* New York: Wiley, 1969.

Mischel, W. *Personality and assessment.* New York: Wiley, 1968.

Mussen, P. H., Conger, J. J., & Kagan, J. *Child development and personality.* New York: Harper & Row, 1969.

Nihlén, K. *Samspelet mellan hem och skola.* Lund: Gleerups, 1976.

Olofsson, B. *Om kriminellt och konformt beteende bland skolpojkar.* Stockholm: Utbildningsförlaget, 1971.

Olweus, D. *Prediction of aggression.* On the basis of a projective test. Skandinaviska Testförlaget, 1969.

Olweus, D. Personality and aggression. In J. K. Cole & D. D. Jensen (Eds.), *Nebraska symposium on motivation 1972.* Lincoln, Neb.: University of Nebraska Press, 1973. (a)

Olweus, D. *Hackkycklingar och översittare. Forskning om skolmobbning.* Stockholm: Almqvist & Wiksell, 1973. (b)

Olweus, D. Personality factors and aggression: With special reference to violence within the peer group. In J. de Wit & W. W. Hartup (Eds.), *Determinants and origins of aggressive behavior.* The Hague: Mouton Press, 1974.

Olweus, D. Development of a multi-faceted aggression inventory for boys. *Reports from the Institute of Psychology,* University of Bergen, Norway, 1975, No. 6.

Olweus, D. *Longitudinal studies of aggression: A review.* Paper presented at the 21st International Congress of Psychology, Paris, July 1976.

Olweus, D. Aggression and peer acceptance in adolescent boys: Two short-term longitudinal studies of ratings. *Child Development,* 1977, *48,* 978–987(a).

Olweus, D. A. critical analysis of the "modern" interactionist position. In D. Magnusson & N. S. Endler (Eds.), *Personality at the cross-roads: Current issues in interactional psychology.* Hillsdale, N.J.: Lawrence Erlbaum Associates, 1977(b).

O'Neal, E. C. & McDonald, P. J. The environmental psychology of aggression. In R. G. Geen & E. C. O'Neal (Eds.), *Perspectives on aggression.* New York: Academic Press, 1976.

Øygarden, S. Lunde, O., & Jørgensen, H. *Grisgrendtprosjeket: Trivsel og tilpasning i ulike ungdomsskolemiljø.* Unpublished paper, 1971.

Patterson, G. R. Behavioral intervention procedures in the classroom and in the home. In A. E. Bergin & S. L. Garfield (Eds.), *Handbook of psychotherapy and behavior change.* New York: Wiley, 1971.

Patterson, G. R. The aggressive child: Architect and victim of a coercive system. In E. J. Marsh, L. A. Hamerlynck, & L. C. Hanley (Eds.), *Behavior modification and families.* New York: Brunner/Mazel, 1975.

Patterson, G. R., Reid, J. B., Jones, R. E., & Conger, R. E. *A social learning approach to family intervention* (Vol. 1). Eugene, Ore.: Castalia, 1975.

Pikas, A. *Så stoppar vi mobbning.* Stockholm: Prisma, 1975.

Powers, E., & Witmer, H. *An experiment in the prevention of delinquency.* New York: Columbia University Press, 1950.

Redl, F., & Wineman, D. *The aggressive child.* New York: Free Press, 1957.

Robins, L. N. *Deviant children grown up.* Baltimore: Williams & Wilkins, 1966.

Russell, W., & Russel, C. Violence, monkeys and man. London: Macmillan, 1968.

Sarason, I. G., & Ganzer, V. J. Modeling and group discussion in the rehabilitation of juvenile delinquents. *Journal of Counseling Psychology,* 1973, *20,* 442-449.

Schjelderup-Ebbe, T. Beiträge zur Sozialpsychologie des Haushuhns. *Zeitschrift für Psychologie,* 1922, *88,* 225-252.

Scott, J. P. *Aggression.* Chicago: University of Chicago Press, 1958.

Sechrest, L. Studies in classroom atmosphere. *Psychology in the Schools,* 1964, *1,* 103-118.

Shaw, M. E. *Group dynamics.* New York: McGraw-Hill, 1971.

Sjölund, A. *Gruppsykologi.* Stockholm: Rabén & Sjögren, 1972.

Staub, E. The learning and unlearning of aggression. In J. L. Singer (Ed.), *The control of aggression and violence.* New York: Academic Press, 1971.

Storr, A. *Human aggression.* New York: Atheneum, 1968.

Tait, C. D., & Hodges, E. F. *Delinquents, their families, and the community.* Springfield, Ill.: Charles C Thomas, 1962.

Thorndike, R. L. The effect of interval between test and retest on the constancy of the I.Q. *Journal of Educational Psychology,* 1933, *24,* 543–549.

Thouless, R. H. The effects of errors of measurement on correlation coefficients. *British Journal of Psychology,* 1939, *29,* 383–403.

Wachtel, P. L. Psychodynamics, behavior therapy, and the implacable experimenter: An inquiry into the consistency of personality. *Journal of Abnormal Psychology,* 1973, *83,* 324–334.

Wahler, R. G. Setting generality, some specific and general effects of child behavior therapy. *Journal of Applied Behavior Analysis,* 1969, *2,* 239–246.

Walder, L. O., Abelson, R. P., Eron, L. D., Banta, T. J., & Laulicht, J. H. Development of a peer-rating measure of aggression. *Psychological Reports,* 1961, *9,* 497–556.

Wallen, N. E., & Travers, R. M. W. Analysis and investigation of teaching methods. In N. L. Gage (Ed.), *Handbook of research on teaching.* Chicago: Rand McNally, 1963.

Watson, R. I. *Psychology of the child.* New York: Wiley, 1965.

West, D. J., & Farrington, D. P. *The delinquent way of life.* London: Heinemann, 1976.

White, R. K., & Lippitt, R. *Autocracy and democracy: An experimental inquiry.* New York: Harper & Row, 1960.

Wiggins, J. S. *Personality and prediction: Principles of personality assessment.* Reading, Mass.: Addison-Wesley, 1973.

Williams, J. F., Meyerson, L. J., Eron, L. D., & Semler, I. J. Peer-rated aggression and aggressive responses elicited in an experimental situation. *Child Development,* 1967, *38,* 181–190.

Winer, B. J. *Statistical principles in experimental design* (2nd ed). New York: McGraw-Hill, 1971.

AUTHOR INDEX

SUBJECT INDEX

211

194